Getting Back
to the
GARDEN

Kenneth Beesecker

ISBN 978-1-64191-407-9 (paperback)
ISBN 978-1-64191-408-6 (digital)

Christian Faith Publishing, Inc.
832 Park Avenue
Meadville, PA 16335
www.christianfaithpublishing.com

Printed in the United States of America

Contents

Foreword

This book is a compilation of mine in my studying of the Word of God, the Bible. It has been completely and totally given to me through the Holy Spirit of our Father, God. It is God-breathed and given.

I have used some ideas and statements from others in the Christian community such as Andrew Wommack, Charles Capps, Bill Winston, Billy Graham, Creflo Dollar, Jack Taylor, Jack Graham, Joyce Meyer, Joseph Prince, Charles Stanley, Robert Morris, Jerry Savelle, Ed Young, John F. Robinson (Mr. Praise Jesus), and Paul Young, author of *The Shack* (see "The Trinity" chapter 3 in this book).

The scriptures, all sixty-six books of the Bible, point to Jesus, the Word of God, the second Person of the Trinity. God has proven his love for mankind from the beginning of time. In Genesis, after the fall of mankind in the Garden, God said, "I will provide the sacrifice, the lamb, my own Son, Jesus, to save the world from sin and death." How can a loving Father not love and care for his children? God is not mad or angry with us. He loves us whether we are good or bad. It's not how much we love God and Jesus; the real key is how much they love us.

Getting Back to the Garden is meant to point and show people biblical truths of why it is so important for us to get born again. Some of these biblical truths are hidden or not really evident to many. This book is meant to give encouragement, knowledge, and understanding of how the Word of God has been imparted to every truly born-again Christian to carry out, live, and manifest this Word in their lives.

This is a quote from my dear brother in Christ, John F. Robinson, Mr. Praise Jesus.

> It's very important the type of seed that I sow, whether it be the corruptible, destructive, ungodly seed from the spirit of this world, the Devil, or the incorruptible good seed of God and all His promises that are fully established in Heaven, to give me God's daily best. For I know for a fact, that I'm fully accountable for the thoughts that I choose to think, and the things which I declare from my mouth. They are sown into my heart willing by me and no one else, making me totally responsible for what the seeds that I sow produce; and knowing that I can't avoid the law of reaping what I sow, I choose to sow only the incorruptible seed of all God's established promises into the heart of my garden and I reap a daily harvest of hundredfold blessings.

The Garden of Eden was God's perfect garden for mankind, and everything in the Garden has a seed to make it alive and living. Even Adam has a seed within him to make and produce life. Father God made the garden, man, and the earth, to give life.

Jesus made it very clear in the scriptures that the Word of God is a seed, and this seed is spoken, written, and inspired by the Holy Spirit. The seed is God, Jesus, a lamp (light), the truth, the way, the life, eternal, and living.

My sincere hope is that you will absorb the words and statements in this book as a valuable tool for your knowledge and understanding for you to be able to use this resource for witnessing and sharing God's Word of truth to others who are in need of a healing physically, emotionally, and spiritually for their lives. Knowledge plus wisdom equals understanding.

I pray that this book will enlighten you, bless you, and show you how much our Father loves you. Hellfire was not made for mankind. It was created for the devil and his fallen angels. Only sinful and unrepentant mankind will send themselves to the lake of fire. Our Father God does not want anyone to perish eternally.

1

In the Beginning

The word *Genesis* means beginning. Chapter 1, verse 1 says, "In the beginning, God created the heavens and the earth." The Lord God, the Creator, made the universe and the earth possibly millions of years ago, or just maybe only six thousand years ago.

There is no such thing as time with God. He made time for mankind because He knew we would need time and seasons to regulate our lives. God said, "Universe be," and it was. All was darkness, void, nothing, and from nothing, the universe became matter—first the spiritual and then the natural.

God spoke everything into existence, and his Word is within himself, a part of him. It was to become His Son Jesus when he spoke himself as sperm into Mary's womb to impregnate her with the baby Jesus. The Word of God creates what it has spoken. Proverbs 18:21 says, "Death and life are in the power of the tongue." In Deuteronomy 30:14, 15, 19, God said, "See, I have set before you today life and prosperity, and death and adversity, the blessing and the curse. So, choose life in order that you may live, you and your descendants." The Lord tells us the consequences of doing right or wrong and then gives us the solution; just choose the right thing to do!

I must interject something here. God does not and never will impose his will or control over mankind in any way. Just as he told Cain, who later killed his brother, Abel, out of jealousy, "if you do what is right, will it not go well with you?" Notice that God said *if*, and there was not yet a law that said, "Thou shall not kill." So Cain was not subject to being put to death for killing his brother, even though it was a sin. God said, "If you do what is right." This means that he did not know if Cain would repent or be a changed or better person because of his wrongdoing. Cain, as a being made in God's image and likeness, had his own free will or choice to make.

John 1:1–3 says, "In the beginning, even before the universe, was the Word, who is Jesus, and the Word was with God. He was in the beginning with (in) God. All things came into being by Him (Jesus the Word), and apart from Him, nothing came into being that was come into being. In Him (Jesus) was life and the life was the light of man. And the Word became flesh and lived among us, and we beheld His glory, from the Father, full of grace and truth."

Light and darkness, as far as illumination is concerned, are both the same to God in the natural sense, but in the spiritual sense, they are good and evil. The Bible says that God is pure light, all good, and loving.

In Genesis 1:3, God said, "Light be." When He spoke of it, He was declaring and saying, "Life be." God as the Trinity was declaring himself. The Word of God is life, but the light of God is what gives life. The Word and light are one. God spoke, "Light be," so that life could happen as we know and see it (see DNA #5 Phosphorus element). Light is life, his true life, the life that is in the Trinity (the Father, the Son, and the Holy Spirit). The spoken word of God creating is called in today's technological terms voice activated system (VAS).

In Genesis 1:26, God said, "Let us make man in our image, in our likeness." Father God, our Creator, was basically talking to himself in the Trinity as "us" and "our." He then gave mankind authority, power, and dominion over every living thing on earth. All living things—the birds, the fish, the animals, and the insects and crawling things—were created by God's voice (VAS) in five days. The sixth day, God made man from the dust or clay of the earth as a potter would do. The seventh day, God rested from his work. He wasn't weary or tired. He wanted us mankind to rest one day a week. He wanted us to also enter his rest, for he knew mankind would need a day of rest (the Sabbath). The love of our Father God is a peace and a rest to our souls.

Seven is the number for perfection. God saw that everything he created was good and perfect in the Garden of Eden. Hebrews 4:11 says, "We are to labor or work to enter God's rest." God has prepared for us a place for rest. We are to rest in the finished work of His Son, Jesus. Just moments before He died on the cross of love, he said, "It is finished." His perfect love is our rest (peace).

In Genesis 2:19–20, God brought the beasts, the birds, the fish, and all the creatures to Adam to see what he would call them. They are all still called by the names Adam gave them to this day. Man was originally given creative power and ability by God at creation. Adam had his own voice activated system within himself given to him by God who created him in his own likeness. And Adam and Eve were created as supernatural beings by God. Hebrews 2:5–8 says God did not give subjection, authority, or dominion of the world to angels. All things on this earth are in subjection and under mankind's feet.

God is a free moral agent and does not and will not impose or force his will on anyone. So when God created mankind, He had to make them also free moral agents with a free will or choice. He had to allow mankind to either accept or reject him.

Adam's name means many (plural). The Hebrew word is *adamah* or *damute*, meaning reddish color from the earth (dust). Adam was the exact blood duplication of God, his Father. God made Adam like a potter makes a clay pot, vessel, or sculpture. Adam had no life in himself when God finished fashioning him. God breathed into Adam's nostrils and mouth his own

Spirit life. This breath of God is called Spirit and is air, oxygen, DNA. The oxygen (air) made blood to flow in Adam's veins and body, and his heart started beating. And the Bible says, "And Adam became a living being, alive." The Bible says that the life of the flesh is in the blood. Blood is life, and our bodies will not live and exist without oxygen, which makes our blood flow and heart beat and flow to the brain and throughout our bodies. Blood is the most precious thing in God's eyes because it is from him, and is a part of him that was given to mankind to have life.

DNA

A   B

DNA: *A* molecular model, 1 hydrogen, 2 oxygen, 3 carbon in the helical phosphate ester chains, 4 carbon and nitrogen in the cross-linked purine and pyrimidine bases, 5 phosphorus: *B* double helix

From *Webster's Collegiate Dictionary* (1979, page 332)
DNA—deoxyribonucleic acid

deo/xy/ribo/nucleic/	acid - composed of sugar base
God/xy-male/rib/RNA-DNA/	phosphoric acid found in cell nuclei
/xx-female/cell/center/	(combines the elements)

This is scientific proof that God created man in his image and likeness.

The DNA contains:

1. Hydrogen—used in synthesis
2. Oxygen—in everything on earth
3. Carbon in the helical phosphate chain/the spiral helix—an acid (salt or ester)
4. Nitrogen—(in 78% of the atmosphere) carbon in the cross linked purine (crystalline base uric acid) and pyrimidine bases (cytosine thymine or uracil)
5. Phosphorus—one that shines or glows in the dark

These five elements have no life in themselves. Only when they are combined together do they give life.

Science has now shown us that at the very moment the sperm of the man penetrates the egg of the woman, there is a spark of light. I believe that this is part of the transference of the DNA of the sperm to the woman into her egg in the uterus. The number 5 element, phosphorus light, is the spark. The Greek word *phos* from the word *phosphorus* means light and means never having to be kindled to start or can never be extinguished or put out. King David said in Psalm 27:1, "The Lord is my light and my salvation, whom shall I fear." The Hebrew word for light is *owr*, and this Hebrew word means a different kind of light than is in the luminaries of the universe, such as stars and suns. *Owr* signifies life as opposed to death.

Today science has shown this to us even further by identifying Laminin. Mankind has more than 37.2 trillion cells in their body: epithelial cells (skin), muscle cells, nerve cells, and connecting tissue cells. A cell consists of a nucleus and cytoplasm and is contained within the cell membrane, which regulates what passes in and out. The nucleus controls the production of proteins. It contains chromosomes, which are the cell's genetic material, and a nucleolus, which produces ribosomes.

Schematic Structure of Laminin 111:

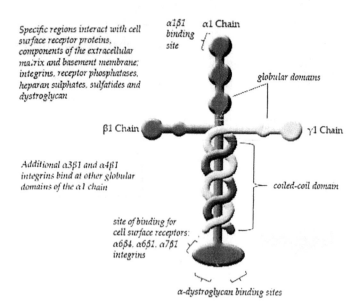

Specific regions interact with cell surface receptor proteins, components of the extracellular matrix and basement membrane; integrins, receptor phosphatases, heparan sulphates, sulfatides and dystroglycan

α1β1 binding site

α1 Chain

globular domains

β1 Chain

γ1 Chain

Additional α3β1 and α4β1 integrins bind at other globular domains of the α1 chain

coiled-coil domain

site of binding for cell surface receptors: α6β4, α6β1, α7β1 integrins

α-dystroglycan binding sites

Laminin is the glue that holds these cells together so that we don't fall into 37.2 trillion pieces. As you will see, the laminin is what keeps our body's cells healthy. When you look at laminin in a telescope, they each individually look like a spiral helix of DNA, but they are shaped like a cross. Thus we have 37.2 trillion laminin or spiral helix crosses binding each of our 37.2 trillion cells together.

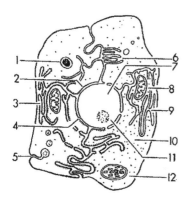

a schematic cell 4: *1* lysosome, *2* nuclear membrane, *3* endoplasmic reticulum with associated ribosomes, *4* nuclear pore, *5* intrusion of cell membrane, *6* Golgi apparatus, *7* nucleus, *8* mitochondrion, *9* endoplasmic reticulum, *10* cytoplasm and ribosomes, *11* nucleolus, *12* chloroplast

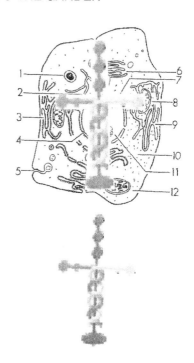

The human cell has twelve components (see diagram #2). The seventh in the center is the nucleus. A prion is an infectious particle and is a cell that does not have a nucleus. Therefore, it is a maverick cell that is dead or malignant that can cause cancer (carcinoma). The invasion of the malignant cells through the basement membrane is a critical step in local infiltration and metastasis. Adhesion and invasion of malignant cells may be modulated by their receptor mediated binding to the basement membrane glycoprotein laminin. The major cell adhesion domain of laminin was localized in the central part of the cross-shaped molecule.

The interaction of malignant cells with basement membranes plays an important role in their metastatic spread. Invasive carcinomas, including colorectal carcinomas, are characterized by the loss of an intact basement membrane. Basement membranes are electron dense twenty to one hundred nm thick layers of which collagen type IV, heparan sulfate proteoglycan, nidogen, and laminin are the major known components. These properties of laminin are related to its potential for cell binding. Heparin, heparan sulfate proteoglycan, and nidogen are what makes the cell and laminin healthy.

In the cross-shaped structure of laminin, each of the A- and B- forms one short arm, and the rest of the three chains together project down the long arm. Immunological, electronmicroscopical, and cell culture studies with laminin fragments have shown that the central part of the molecule is responsible for cell adhesion. In addition to promoting cell adhesion, central fragments of laminin also decrease the metastatic potential of tumor cells presumably by saturation of laminin receptors thought to be involved in tumor cell invasion through basement membranes. Thus, the terminal part on the long arm contains a heparin binding domain, and the distal end of the long arm has been recognized to have a high affinity cell domain, which stimulates cell spreading.

An antibody is a protein that surrounds the cells and stops the cancer or infection from growing, and it is the memory cell that carries the memory of how to overcome the specified virus. Jesus's blood carries the antibody of how he defeated sin—chokes it and kills it; death gives life. The blood of Jesus is liquid love, and it has the power to remove your sin from the memory of God.

The woman does not give the life to the fetus. She incubates, feeds, and gives fluids to the fetus. The fetus already has its life in the sperm transfer of the male to the egg of the woman. This is a blood transfer into the egg of the woman. The man's sperm is a DNA transfer and has XY chromosomes (male and female). Whichever one penetrates the egg makes the male or female child. The fetus (baby) scientifically has the father's blood.

When God placed himself into mother Mary's womb, it was a blood transfer biblically called spermos (sperm). Baby

Jesus had God's blood, not the blood from a human man. The Aramaic and Hebrew word for blood is *dam* (when someone says to another person, "Damn you," they are putting a curse by their words upon that person's blood or, in essence, God's blood).

Adam and Eve were created as supernatural beings. They were created as a triune or tripart being, similar to the Trinity, perfect in body, soul, and spirit. At the fall in the Garden of Eden, Adam and Eve lost the glory of God, the super part of their supernatural being. They lost the divine nature of their Father God. In 2 Peter 1:3, 4, it says, "His divine power has granted to us everything pertaining to life and godliness through the true knowledge of Him who called us by His own glory and excellence. He has granted to us to become partakers of the divine nature."

The first and only rule or law given to man was, "Don't eat of this one tree," in the midst of maybe hundreds or maybe thousands of trees in the garden. This one tree was called the Tree of knowledge. Adam and Eve were originally vegetarians. They didn't eat meat. There was also a tree in the garden called the Tree of life. Adam and Eve were allowed to eat of all the trees, even the Tree of life, but not of the Tree of knowledge.

This Tree of life is the Word of God, Jesus Christ. When Jesus was here on earth with us, he said, "Abide in me, and I in you. As the branch cannot bear fruit of itself, unless it abides in the vine. I am the vine and you (we) are the branches; he who abides in Me, and I in him, he bears much fruit" (John 15:4–7). The true source of life comes from the root (God) to the tree (vine—Jesus) to the branches (us). The fruit is born or comes from the branches, but the life of the fruit is in the root. Jesus said, "I am the way, the truth, and the life; no one comes to the Father (the root) but through me" (John 14:6). John 10:10 says, "I have come that you may have life and have it more abundantly."

To abide in Christ as a branch abides in the vine is to live a life of communion, and the life of the vine is the life of the branches. We are the branches and the branch and vine form one existence. Jesus said in the high priestly prayer, "And the glory which you, Father, have given me, I have given them, that they may be one just as we are one" (John 17:22). The unity for which Christ prays is no mere quality of our life in Christ; it is our only life in Christ, and this unity (communion) is the very life of salvation. The only thing the branches (us) have to do is just remain connected to the vine, Jesus, and the fruit will produce.

Now Satan, being more cunning and crafty than all the beasts of the earth, knew that he could persuade Eve more easily than Adam and that when she gave in, she could convince her husband to follow the same course.

The lie of Satan to Eve was actually in the form of a question, which caused her to doubt God the Father. So we can say just as Jesus did that Satan (devil) is a lie, the father of lies, and this first lie is what brought death to the world. He said to Eve, "Did God actually say that you shall not eat of *any* tree in the garden?" She answered, "We may eat of the fruit of the trees, but not the one in the midst of the garden, and neither shall we touch it lest we die." God did not tell them not to touch the tree. Satan then said to her, "You will not surely die. For God knows that when you eat of it, your eyes will be opened, and you will be like God knowing good and evil."

Whatever the fruit may have been, its use was a plain violation of divine prohibition. It was an unwarranted desire for forbidden knowledge. The gravity of the offense consisted not in the act itself but in the fact that Adam and Eve committed it consciously and deliberately against God's explicit and emphatic command.

The fruit of the forbidden Tree of knowledge was *malum*, which means "evil." This word was mistranslated as *malam*, which means "apple." Adam and Eve did evil against God, and if you spell *evil* backwards, it comes out as *live* or to have life. This is what I call to reverse the curse.

God told Adam and Eve that in the day they ate of the fruit of the tree of knowledge, they would surely die. Satan, the devil, knew the heart of God, the all-loving and faithful Father, and knew that he would not let them die physically on the spot. The death that they experienced was the loss of the Holy Spirit of God leaving their beings, the very moment they ate of the tree.

Satan told Eve a lie—that they would be like God, all-powerful, all-knowing, and all-present. The truth was, they were already exactly like God, made in His image and likeness. God's being, his ways and thoughts are so much greater and higher than ours, or Satan, for that matter, and no human or angel can be more than a speck of dust equal to God.

At the fall of Adam and Eve, it was the mind that fell the farthest. Adam and Eve no longer trusted or believed God their Father. Sin is unbelief. They wanted to be independent from God and wanted to do things by their own self-effort and performance by totally rejecting God, and now they had a perceived power and no longer trusted God.

The death that God spoke about was a twofold death. The first and most important death was the loss of the Holy Spirit of God. This was the loss of God's life in them, and the Holy Spirit left their souls. The Holy Spirit is the third person of the Trinity. The second death for them was a physical death of the body. If Adam and Eve had not disobeyed and sinned against God, they would still be alive today, six thousand years later. The moment Adam and Eve sinned, they received a conscience and felt guilt and shame for their disobedience. They lost their confidence in their creator and lost the truth of the Holy Spirit. They became at that moment sin-conscious, just like everyone of us to this day.

Adam and Eve passed the sin, shame, and guilt genetically to all mankind to this day. We didn't do the original sin, but this sin nature was passed on to us and produces the fruit of sin in our lives. God knew that creating mankind in His image and likeness with a free will that they would have the propensity or mind to do their own thing. He didn't know for sure that they would disobey him, but he knew they had the ability to do so. So God, after they fell and sinned, had a backup plan, a plan B. In Genesis 3:15, "I will put enmity between you (Satan) and the woman, and between your seed and her seed; He shall crush you on the head, and you shall bruise Him (Jesus, the Word) on the heel."

There are now to be consequences (punishment) for their sin. Adam was, from the beginning, told to work and keep the garden in good and beautiful shape. But now God said that he would have to work even harder to make a living, and there would now be thorns, thistles, and weeds to contend with. Eve already had discomfort in childbirth, but God said her punishment was to have even greater pain.

Before their fall, Adam and Eve walked and talked with God in the Garden of Eden. At the fall, they lost the knowing, the deep personal intimacy with God their Father. After their sin, they heard God's voice as he was coming to them in the garden. They were afraid and hid themselves from his presence, and they covered themselves with fig leaves, for now they knew sin and nakedness. God knew they were hiding from him in shame and guilt. He said, "Where are you?" (he knew where they were and what they had done). What he was saying to them was, "What is your position and standing now in my creation?"

God, as their all-loving Father, by his mercy (forgiveness) then killed some animals—probably deer, sheep, or cattle— and he personally made clothes to cover their nakedness. This was the very first blood sacrifice for the covering of sin. This was a type and shadow of the Hebrew priests who came to be much later and who would kill the lambs, goats, oxen, etc, and then sprinkle their blood on the mercy seat of the Ark of the

Covenant for the covering and forgiveness of sins for the people and nation of Israel. This act of the sprinkling of the animals' blood and covering of sins could only work for one year and had to be repeated every year by the priests. It only covered the sin and did not completely take away the sin forever.

Four thousand years after the fall of Adam and Eve, when Jesus was crucified on the cross of love, he was the final and ultimate sacrifice for our sins. Jesus's shed blood on the cross totally washed away mankind's sins forevermore, and that was about two thousand years ago. His blood sacrifice is never needed to be repeated and done again ever. His shed blood is a continuing, ongoing, unseen, eternal process to this day for those of us who are truly born-again Christians.

God has totally forgiven and forgotten our sins, and he no longer keeps a record in heaven of a true believer's sins. God has an ability that no man has, and that is to be able to completely not remember a true believer's sins anymore forever.

Before His death and resurrection, Jesus said, "This is eternal life, that you may know the Father and the Son whom he sent." Now our eternal life and salvation must come out of death—death to our own wants, needs, desires, agendas, and rights to the will of God. There is no plan B in here. We must die to our own self-will and get back into us the Holy Spirit of God, into our spirit and soul, by becoming as Jesus said, born-again. (See chapter 15, "Life Comes Out of Death.") This means that we must believe that Jesus is the Son of God born in the flesh, crucified, died and buried, resurrected, and ascended back to heaven for our sins.

Adam and Eve were naked and did not realize it when they were in the garden before the fall. This was because they were clothed with the image, glory, and Holy Spirit of their creator, God. They were supernatural beings.

Glory in the Greek is *doxa*, icon, or image. *Doxa* embraces all which is excellent in the divine nature, coinciding with God's self-revelation. It comprises all that God will appear to be in his final revelation to us. God's glory made itself manifest in and through his Son, Jesus. In John 17:22, 23, Jesus said in the high priestly prayer, "And the glory which you, my Father have given me, I have given them (the apostles and us Christians).

This has to happen in your spirit, heart, and mind first, and then the Holy Spirit comes and lives in your spirit and soul. When you believe and this happens, you are now a supernatural being, just like Adam and Eve, before their fall in the Garden of Eden. You are now "back to the garden," in nature, so to speak.

2

Relationship

God created mankind because he wanted to have a family relationship. God is a relational being as well as a Spirit.

Before their fall in the Garden of Eden, Adam and Eve walked and talked with their Father, the Creator, daily. They had a close and loving relationship.

We see that the three persons of the Trinity are in a constant relationship of love and respect for each other. The Trinity is: the Father, the Son (Jesus), and the Holy Spirit.

Good relationships are never about power, and one way to avoid the will to power is to limit oneself to serve. Humans often do this in touching the infirm and sick, in serving the ones whose minds have left to wander in relation to the poor, in loving the very old and the very young, or even in caring for that "other" who has assumed a position of power over them. Right behavior doesn't produce a right relationship with God. Right relationship with God produces a right behavior, total trust in him, and he can now totally trust us.

Many folks try to grasp some sense of who God is by taking the best version of themselves, projecting that to the nth degree, factoring in all the goodness they can perceive, which often isn't much, and then call that God. The truth is, it falls pitifully short of who he really is. God is above and beyond all that you can ask or think. In Isaiah 55:6–10, God said, "For my thoughts are not your thoughts, neither are your ways my ways." God was not talking about believers here. He was speaking of the unrighteous, not to those who love and obey him.

Created beings can only take what already exists and from it fashion something different. God takes the invisible unseen things and makes them visible. We Christians have been given the same ability by our Father God, voice activated system (VAS), which is our words.

Humans are truly blind to their own place in the creation. Having chosen the ravaged path of independence (Adam and Eve), they don't comprehend that they are dragging the entire creation along with them. Humans declaring good and evil without true knowledge is the tree of knowledge. We humans take it upon ourselves to determine good and evil. We become the judge, and to make things even more confusing, that which we determine to be good and evil, will change over time and circumstance. And beyond that, and even worse, there are billions of people, each determining what is good and what is evil.

So when your good and evil clash with your neighbor's, fights and arguments ensue, and even wars break out. This allows us to play God in our independence, and now there is no longer any relationship. Wanting to be independent is making yourself to be God.

Rights are where survivors go so that they don't have to work out relationships. We must give up our rights to decide what is good and evil on our own terms. Choose only to live in the Holy Spirit, and to do that, we must know the Lord enough to trust him and learn to rest in his inherent goodness.

People are tenacious when it comes to the treasure of their imaginary independence. They hoard and hold their sickness with a firm grasp. They find their identity and worth in their brokenness and guard it with every ounce of strength they have. No wonder that grace has so little attraction to them. And in this sense, they have tried to lock the door of their heart from the inside. We are saints in the hands of a loving God.

Ephesians 2:16, 18 says, "Jesus reconciled us in one body (unity) to God through the cross, by it having put to death the enmity; for through Him (Jesus) we have our access in one Spirit to the Father." Hebrews 10:22 also says, "With a sincere heart, in full assurance of faith, having our hearts sprinkled clean from an evil conscience and our bodies washed with pure water."

The flesh is existence apart from God and is self-reliant rather than God-dependent. It is self-centered rather than Christ-centered.

There is something about Satan that many in the Christian world don't understand. Satan was the highest created angel in heaven. He was called the light bringer, the angel of light. He was the most beautiful and gorgeous of all heaven's angels that God had created. He was the worship leader in heaven. God created all angels by speaking them into existence. He also did this with the animals, birds, fish, etc., but not so with mankind. Mankind was formed and fashioned by God's own hands as a potter does from the dust of the earth (Genesis 2:7).

God, in making and creating mankind in his own image and likeness, had to give man a free will or choice of his own. Thus, mankind can choose to repent of his sin or wrongdoing. Angels cannot repent because they can't understand this, and they marvel at how mankind can do this. The angels were created to obey the Word or voice of God. The Bible says that a man who is born again will rule and be in authority over angels in eternity. Since God, our Father, made us in his image and likeness, this has made Satan jealous and angry because he is not made in God's image and likeness and can never be a begotten son of God. Our creator, God, has given us all authority, dominion, and power on earth.

Satan wants to kill and destroy every man, woman, and child because we are the apple of our Father's eye. God loves us so much that he even died for us to keep us as his own. Satan is jealous also because God has crowned mankind with glory and honor.

3

The Trinity

The Trinity or Godhead is: the Father, the Son, and the Holy Spirit. God says, "Even though you can't grasp Me, I still want to be known. And there are some advantages to being God. By My nature I am completely unlimited and without bounds. I have always known fullness and I live in a state of perpetual satisfaction as My normal state of existence. Then, Adam chose to go it on his own, as We, the Trinity knew he would, and then everything got all messed up. But, instead of scraping the whole creation, We pulled up Our sleeves and entered into the middle of the mess. And that's what We have done in sending the Son, Jesus. When God spoke Himself into human existence, as the Son of God, We became fully human."

This is like a bird whose nature is to fly but choosing only to be grounded. He doesn't stop being a bird, but it does alter his experience of life significantly. So although by nature Jesus is fully God and he is also fully human and lives as such, while never losing the innate ability to fly, he chooses moment by moment to remain grounded, and that is why his name is Immanuel, meaning "God with us."

When Jesus raised the dead to life, healed the blind, and made the cripples walk, he did so as a dependent limited human being, trusting in God's life and power to be at work within him and through him.

The Trinity thing: "We are not three gods and We are not talking about one god with three attitudes; like a man who is a husband, father, and worker. I am one God and I am three person's, and each of the three is fully and entirely One. If I were simply one God and one person then you would find yourself in this creation without something wonderful. You would be without love and relationship. All love and relationship is possible for you because it already exists within Me, the Trinity." Love is not the limitation; love is the flying. "I am love!"

"Do you understand that unless I had an object of love, or more accurately, a someone to love, and if I did not have such a relationship within Myself, then I would not be capable of love at all? You would have a God who could not love. Or, maybe worse, when he chose, could only love as a limitation of his nature." Also, anger for God is an expression of love all the same. He loves the ones he's angry with just as much as those he's not angry with. The God who is the I AM cannot act apart from love.

Love is not a feeling; it is a conscious decision that you make.

The Trinity has no concept of final authority among themselves, only unity. The Trinity is a circle of love and relationship, not a chain of command or a great chain of being. Humans are so lost and damaged that it is almost incomprehensible that people could work or live together without someone being in charge. Once you have hierarchy, you need rules to protect and administer it. And then you need law and enforcement of the rules, and you end up with some kind of chain of command or a system of order that destroys relationship from power. Authority is merely the excuse the strong use to make others conform to what they want.

When you choose independence over relationship, you become a danger to one another. Creation has gone down a very different path than what the Lord has desired. In the world, the value of the individual is constantly weighed against the survival of the system, whether political, economic, social, or religious—any system actually. First, one person and then a few, and finally many are sacrificed for the good and ongoing existence of the system. This lies behind every struggle for power, every prejudice, every war, and every abuse of relationship. Mankind, as the crowning glory of creation, made in the image of the Trinity was to be unencumbered by structure and to be free to simply *be* in relationship with the Lord and one another.

Lost and now damaged, to mankind, it is almost incomprehensible that relationship could exist apart from hierarchy. So we think that God must relate inside a hierarchy also, but he does not.

The Trinity wants to share their love, joy, freedom, and light (life) that they already know within themselves. Mankind was created to be in face-to-face relationship with the Lord and to join in the Trinity's circle of love. Fallen humans are the ones who embrace fear, pain, and rights so readily in relationships.

As difficult as it is to understand, everything that has taken place and is occurring is exactly according to God's purpose without violating choice or will. Our choices are not stronger than the Lord's purposes.

Our lives are like a messy garden, a fractal which is something considered simple and orderly, and that is actually composed of repeated patterns no matter how magnified; a fractal is almost infinitely complex. Broken humans center their lives around things that seem good to them but will neither fill them nor free them. When disaster happens, these same people will turn against the false powers they trusted. In their disappointment, either they become softened toward God or they become bolder in their own independence.

God does love us, and he is not justifying, He is redeeming and restoring us. Freedom involves trust and obedience inside a relationship of love. The choice to eat of the forbidden tree tore the universe apart, divorcing the spiritual from the physical or material. They died expelling in the breath of their choice, the very breath of God.

The Holy Spirit is the Spirit of Jesus, the Son. It is creativity, action, and the breathing of life. God the Father is El, as Creator, and is truly real and the ground of all being.

Humans are where they were always intended to be—in the center of the Trinity's love and purpose, in perfect relationship.

4

Your True Identity

The Bible is a mirror of who you are. You can't see your spirit, and there is nothing in the natural that can touch your spirit. The Bible is your true reflection, and it's the freedom of grace, which is the image of Jesus in us. Romans 8:16, 17 says, "The Holy Spirit with our spirit assures us that we are sons and daughters of God, co-heirs with Christ."

New Testament is image or icon, and the Old Testament is shadow. Time is not linear but shaped, revealed, and given its meaning by its end. Thus, the truth who is Christ himself is not trapped within the confines of history. Truth has encountered history and made himself manifest in that moment, but the same truth, as the end of all things, is free and able to make himself manifest at every moment and at all time. We are not defined by our history but by our end. To know what we are, it is necessary to know what we shall be.

In John 4:24, Jesus said, "God is Spirit, and those who worship Him, must worship in Spirit and truth." Genesis 2:7 says, "Then the Lord God formed man of dust from the ground and breathed into his nostrils the breath of life (spirit); and man became a living being (soul)." In 1 Corinthians 15:45, it also says, "The first Adam became a living soul, the last Adam (Jesus), became a life giving Spirit." At creation, mankind became another speaking spirit, just like their Father God. The spirit of man cannot die physically. "He who is joined to the Lord is one Spirit." God put his Spirit into man, a physical fleshly body, and gave humans sight, smell, taste, touch, and hearing so that they could know others in the natural or physical realm.

The inward man, the spirit, has not been revealed to the natural or soulish man. You must identify with God that you are a spirit being housed in the skin of a physical body. "God is Spirit, and I am a spirit."

Romans 8:6 says, "A carnal (fleshly) mind is death and is dominated by the five senses; sight, smell, taste, touch, and hearing." Carnal means "of the five senses." Carnality produces sickness, disease, depression, stress, and anxiety. All sin is carnality, but not all carnality is sin. If your mind is dominated by your senses, you are of the world. You can be born again and not have power, dominion, and authority on this earth. If your mind tells you that you can't see the spiritual, you won't believe the spiritual. Don't make a god out of your mind and reasoning! You have to receive the truths of God in order to be saved and born again.

One common denominator for all struggling Christians is they do not know who they are in Christ, nor do they understand what it means to be a child of God. Romans 8:16 says, "The Spirit Himself bears witness with our spirit that we are children of God." The root of bad behavior is not realizing in your spirit that you are God's child. Identity theft goes back to Adam and Eve in the Garden of Eden. Adam lost his identity to who he was as God's son. Satan legally stole Adam's original image and likeness of God.

Ultimately, however, every Christian is responsible for his or her own maturity and freedom in Christ. Nobody can make you grow. That's your decision and daily responsibility. You alone must follow through with that process. The grace walk is living by faith in the power of the Holy Spirit.

You are already a whole person and possess a life of infinite meaning and purpose because of who you are—a child of God.

The only identity equation that works in God's kingdom is you plus Christ equals wholeness and meaning. We Christians fail, so we see ourselves as failures, which only leads to more failure. We sin, so we see ourselves as sinners, which only leads to more sin. God wants us to know that as a child of God who is alive and free in Christ, this should determine what we do.

Bios describes the union of your physical body and your immaterial self—mind, emotions, and will. To be physically alive means the soul or soul/spirit (zoos) is in union with your body. To die physically means that you are separated from your temporal body. Your immaterial inner self needs your outer self to live and function in this world.

The spiritual life of the believer doesn't age or decay as does the outer shell. To be spiritually alive is the word *zoe*, which means that your soul or soul/spirit is in union with God, and that is the condition in which Adam was created—physically alive and spiritually alive and in perfect union with God.

This spiritual life means being in Christ or in him. Adam sinned and severed his union with God, but God's eternal plan was to bring human creation back to himself (restoration), the union he enjoyed with Adam at creation and today is called born again. Adam had a sense of significance and enjoyed a sense of safety and security. Adam was completely cared for in the garden.

The effects of the fall were dramatic, immediate, and far-reaching, infecting every subsequent member of the human race (Romans 5:12, 1 Corinthians 15:21, 22), and every human being is born physically alive but spiritually dead, separated from God (Ephesians 2:1).

The world system is what it is. Institutions, systems, ideologies, and all the vain futile efforts of humanity that go with them are everywhere, and interaction with all of it is unavoidable. But Jesus gives us freedom to overcome any system of power in which we find ourselves, be it religious, social, economic, or political.

A spiritual mind is life and peace. Jesus said, "The words I speak to you, they are Spirit and they are life." Spiritual-mindedness is a mind dominated by the Word of God, which is the Bible.

Peace, which is an emotion, is linked to how and what you think. You have no peace because your mind is still fixed on the problems. Circumstances shouldn't cause you to lose your peace. You need your soul, which is your mind, will, and emotions attached to the Word of God. You can't draw out God's peace in your spirit when it is dominated by your senses.

The Bible defines you as a new creature or creation when you are born again. Take time out to realize who you are. "I'm a child of, or, a son or daughter of God, created in the image of God and I'm like Jesus and He lives in me." Is Jesus broke? No! Does Jesus sin? No! Is Jesus full of disease, crippled, or sick? No! Tell yourself this, "I have the mind of Jesus Christ, and he lives in me."

John 1:14–17 says, "Jesus, the Word, became flesh like us. Being full of grace and truth, and of His fullness we have received grace for grace, grace for grace, upon grace, upon grace…" This is what I call a gracelet, wrapped around my wrist forever.

In 2 Corinthians 5:17, it says, "If any man is in Christ, he is a new creature or creation; the old things passed away, now all things have become new." Galatians 2:20 also says, "I have been crucified with Christ, and it is no longer I who live, but Christ lives in me, and the life we now live, we live by the faith of Jesus Christ." Ephesians 2:6, 7 says, "God raised us up with Jesus and seated us with Him in the heavenly places in Christ Jesus." In 1 John 4:17, it says, "As He (Jesus) is right now, so are we believers in this world." We came from heaven, and we are to walk as Christ on this earth. We should be doing unlimited demonstrations, miraculous activities, and manifestations as the body of Christ. We have God's Spirit without measure, with no limitations.

We Christians have the same DNA spiritually as God and Jesus Christ, and God put into Christ everything he wanted us to be. We are literally made holy by our identification with Christ. The Apostle Paul talks about us being in Christ about 160 times in the New Testament.

Affirmations

I will grow in freedom to be inside or outside all kinds of systems and to move freely between and among them. Inside me, I have the wisdom of God, and I declare it by the Word of God. I have acknowledged this fact, and it is now released in me and out of me. I am Jesus's little brother, a twin to him, adopted into the family of God, a coheir with him. I am perfect, pure, blameless, and seated with him and the Father in the heavenly realm right now.

I am tied to Jesus's identity. My victory and success in life comes from Jesus, and I am anointed just like him. We are to think the same way as Christ. I have the mind of Christ, and I have His authority and power in me through the Holy Spirit. The real me is Spirit, and as he is in heaven at the right hand of God, so am I in this world. I am the righteousness of God in Christ Jesus. The Gospel of Jesus Christ is an expression of light, and my light is the light that overwhelms the darkness in this world.

We are the New Testament temple, considered holy, and within us is the holy place of God.

5

Renewing Your Mind

Repentance means to change the way that you think. Once we are engaged to renewing our mind, we must learn to release what we already have: healing, deliverance, and abundance.

When you change your thinking and change your attitude, this will change your behavior. This is especially true for many people today.

Mankind is a spirit being. He possesses a soul, and he lives in a physical or material body. We are spirit beings, not a body. You are a spirit, you have a soul, and you live in a body. The soul is your mind, will, and emotions. The spirit possesses the soul compartment and at death leaves your body, and your body decays. Your spirit changes when you are born again.

It says in 2 Corinthians 5:17 that in Christ we are a new creature, a totally new creation. Something totally different. Before we were born again, our spirit was dead to God and in sin. Now, being born again, you became a new species of being. Now the real you is a being that never existed before. When you became born again, the only part of you that was impacted was your spirit and soul (mind). Now you need to renew or reprogram your mind.

The Christian Walk

The Apostle Paul is writing to the Ephesian church in chapter 4, verses 17 to 32. In verses 17 to 19, he is telling them not to walk and live their lives like the Gentiles (non-Jews). In verse 20 to 21, he says, "But you did not learn Christ in this way, if you were truly born-again in Him." Verse 22 says in reference to your former manner of life, you must lay aside the *old self*, which is being corrupted in accordance with the lust of deceit, and that you be renewed in the *spirit of your mind* and put on the *new self*, which in the likeness of God has been created in righteousness and holiness of the truth.

Therefore, laying aside falsehood, speak truth, each one of you with his neighbor, for we are members of one another. Be angry and do not sin. Do not let the sun go down on your anger, and do not give the devil an opportunity. Let him who steals steal no longer, but rather let him labor, performing with his own hands what is good, in order to share with him who has needs.

Let no unwholesome word proceed from your mouth but only such a word that is good for edification, according to need, that it may give grace to those who hear. And do not grieve the Holy Spirit of God, by whom you were sealed, for the day of redemption. Let all bitterness and wrath and anger and clamor and slander be put away from you, along with all malice (wickedness as an evil habit). And be kind to one another, tender-hearted, forgiving each other, just as God in Christ has also forgiven you.

Chapter 5, verses 1 to 5 says to be imitators of God as beloved children, and walk in love, just as Christ also loved you. But do not let immorality or impurity or greed even be named among you, as is proper among saints; there must be no filthiness and silly talk or coarse jesting. No immoral or impure person or covetous man, who is an idolater, has an inheritance in the kingdom of Christ and God.

Romans 12:2 says, "Do not be conformed to this world, but be transformed or changed by the renewing of your mind, so that you may prove what the will of God is, that which is good and acceptable and perfect." I wanted to know what it meant by "that which is good and acceptable and perfect." It took me a few minutes, and I found it in 1 Thessalonians 4:3, "For this is the will of God, your sanctification (purity); that is, that you *abstain from sexual immorality.*"

The old school of teaching and science used to say that our minds after the age of maybe two just remains the same and doesn't change. This is not so anymore. Scientists have proven that our mind is always changing, even into old age, and this is called mapping.

In 1 Peter 1:14–16, it says, "As obedient children do not be conformed to the former lusts which were yours in your ignorance, but like the Holy One who called you, be holy yourselves also in your behavior; because it is written, 'You shall be Holy, for I am Holy.'"

The enemy comes in to introduce another mind set to us about a thing. This is called being double-minded (James 1:7, 8). When your mind is renewed with the Word of God, it's renewed with the new creation. Now your spirit is in agreement with your soul (mind, will, emotions). Now you realize and know that God is in you, with you, and one Spirit with you. We have got to become like-minded with God (conscious). You are no longer in the process of trying to get something from God. Everything you ever need for this life as a Christian is already in you and in its entirety. You already have the fullness of Christ in you.

The Bible is now a mirror into the realm of the Spirit. The Word (the Bible) is a reflection showing me my spirit and is a mirror of God. You can't see what's in your spirit; his Word is the mirror. The expiration date is today, and the enemy (Satan) has no more control in your life.

Affirmation

I choose to set my mind on only the true spiritual laws of God. Now the Holy Ghost (Spirit) and my spirit make something awesome to happen in my life. And now my spirit and soul are against what my body wants to do. I'm not of this world. I'm in it, but I'm not a part of this system. God said, "Everything you need I already gave to you, and it's inside you." Amen!

The word *Amen* is originally an Aramaic word and is also used in the Hebrew language. It means "sealed in truth."

6

Releasing What Is Yours

Most Christians have their reality based on their own intellect, logic, and reasoning. This is not true of God. Most Christians don't have a true revelation of the Holy Spirit. When your spirit agrees with your soul, that's two against one. Now your body needs to come into agreement. Your spirit is the life-giving force, and it is the core and the real you. In your spirit, you have the same power that raised Jesus from the dead, and it is possible for you to have this power and never manifest it. It's when your mind (soul part) doesn't agree with the Word of God.

You can actually die with all the power that raised Jesus from the dead, sitting untapped within you. It's like a person dying of thirst with a pitcher in their hand while sitting next to a well of water.

Your body doesn't control anything. It just goes with the flow of what it sees, by what it touches, tastes, smells, and hears unless you influence it with your mind.

The Christian life is not about getting from God. He already gave the best, his only begotten Son, Jesus, on the cross of love. The Christian life is a process of renewing your mind and learning how to use what you have already received from God. God has already promised you healing, joy, peace, and prosperity. You already have it all. The Word of God says that we are to capture every thought to the obedience of Christ. Let your light shine and be the light of God to the world. Jesus told us that we are the light of the world and the salt of the earth.

So I can declare by Jesus's authority given to me, "I am the light and love, and there is no darkness in me." Light, love, and life actually exist. So removing yourself from the Lord will plunge you into darkness. Declaring your independence from God will result in evil because apart from the Lord, you can only draw upon yourself, and that is death because you have separated (divorced) yourself from Jesus, the author and finisher of life, the beginning and the end.

Write the word on your heart. Celebrate God's goodness and wonder all around you. Share your blessings and be a living prayer in the world. Proclaim to everyone, "I am greatly blessed, highly favored, and deeply loved, and so are you."

7

"I Am Supernatural"

Jesus died on the cross of love in my place. My physical body has literally died on that cross in the body of Christ Jesus. This is called the great exchange—his death for my death, his life for my life. This is what baptism means and is all about. I am washed totally clean by Jesus's blood. "I have been crucified with Christ, and it is now no longer I who live, but Christ is in me. He loves me to death" (Galatians 2:20). Romans 6:6 says, "Our old self was crucified with Him, that our body of sin should no longer be slaves to sin. Now if we died with Christ, we believe that we shall also live with Him."

Born once—die twice/Born twice—die once

Romans 8:10 says, "And if Christ is in you, though the body is dead because of sin, yet the Spirit is alive because of righteousness." Galatians 3:27–29 also says, "For all of you who were baptized into Christ, have clothed yourselves with Christ. And if you belong to Christ, then you are Abraham's offspring, heirs according to the Promise."

John 17:13–26 says the night before he was crucified, in the high priestly prayer, Jesus said, "They are not of the world, even as I am not of this world. But I also pray for those who believe in Me through their word, that they may all be one; even as You Father are in Me, and I in Thee, that they also may be in Us; that the world may believe that You sent Me."

Jesus was laid in the Tomb physically dead. On the third day before dawn, on the first day of the week, Jesus was raised back to life by the power of the Holy Spirit. He was resurrected in his physical bodily form. When we are baptized into Jesus's death in the water, we come out of the water a new physical bodily being, alive, just as Christ is alive.

It says in 2 Corinthians 3:17, 18 that now the Lord is the Spirit, and where the Spirit of the Lord is, there is liberty. But we all, with unveiled face beholding as in a mirror the glory of the Lord, are being transformed (metamorphosis) into the same image from glory to glory, just as from the Lord, the Spirit.

Being born again and baptized in the Greek language is called metamorphosis or in the English, transmutation. It is to be changed into a totally new creature, like the caterpillar becoming a beautiful butterfly. It also means to change or alter in appearance or form to a higher nature. "I now have the divine nature of God (DNA)." In 2 Peter 1:4, it says, "We have God's precious and magnificent promises in order that by them we might become partakers of the divine nature." Ephesians 4:13, 24 also says, "The new self, the likeness of God, created in righteousness and holiness of the truth."

The caterpillar worm climbs a tree and wraps a cocoon around itself, and zoologists believe that the caterpillar worm then dies inside the cocoon. In about two weeks, the caterpillar is resurrected into a totally new body as a beautiful butterfly. The butterfly still has the same DNA as when it was a caterpillar worm but has been changed in appearance and form to a higher nature. This is the same thing that happens to us when we get truly born again as a Christian.

Affirmation

My divine nature has been birthed by my Father, God, himself. I am a child of the light. I now have the blood of God. Colossians 3:3–8 says, "I am a dead man walking and I died, and my life is now hidden with Christ in God. I am now a supernatural being just like the Father and His Son Jesus."

Can the butterfly go back to being a worm crawling on its belly again? No! Once we are truly born again as a supernatural son or daughter of God, we can no longer go back to our old fallen, sinful, nature. As the butterfly was transformed from a worm to a beautiful butterfly, so are we. The butterfly no longer even thinks of itself as a lowly worm anymore. We are to be transformed into our supernatural nature by the renewing of our mind (Romans 12:2; 1 Peter 1:14).

Our spiritual heart must tell our mind that we are a new creature or creation. God is a triune being, and he made us as a triune being. Example: Father, Son, Holy Spirit (Trinity); mankind—body, soul, and spirit. The renewing of our mind is taking on the mind of Christ, which is a divine sonship, and Jesus in us is the kingdom come. His being born and appearing in this world was not to bring the kingdom only; it was to conclude the kingdom of God, "It is finished."

Colossians 2:6, 8–13 says, "We are now complete in Christ." Can you add to completeness? No! (In 1 Timothy 6:17–19; Hebrews 13) Does Jesus sin? No! In 1 Corinthians 2:16, it says, "We have the mind of Christ, and he and the Father is in us." This is for us Christians to be born again and to the Jewish person who believes in Jesus Christ; they call it "to be completed." If I am in Christ and he is in me, do I sin? Yes! But I am no longer a sinner. I am exactly what Adam and Eve were at creation before their fall—supernatural.

This is my epiphany or revelation from the Holy Spirit:

God made Adam to be the exact blood duplication of himself in body, soul, and spirit. Adam was a supernatural perfect being. Genesis 2:7 said then the Lord formed man of dust from the ground and breathed into his nostrils the breath of life, and man became a living being. When God breathed into Adam's nostrils, it was a blast of air. Spirit in Hebrew is *ruwach*, and in Greek, it is *pneuma*, and they both mean air, wind, and breath. We can correctly say to God, "It's your breath in our lungs, so we pour out our praise to you only."

God is essentially a spirit. Therefore, man, who is similar to God, possesses an immortal or eternal spirit. Man is a person with the power to think, feel, and decide (choice). He has the capacity for moral choices and spiritual growth or decline. The fall in the Garden of Eden reversed this. Mankind was originally righteous but now loves evil more than righteousness. Man is no longer in the perfect state of innocence as at the time of creation. He no longer has the same godlike attributes and qualities of that original state.

Soul means "that which breathes," and it is life, the affections, the will, and the consciousness, while the spirit stood for higher elements by which we comprehend truths. Adam and Eve were originally supernatural beings. Mankind lost the presence of the Holy Spirit. They lost the super part and became natural in all things. We must first believe in Jesus and his name, and we now get the Holy Spirit back into our soul and spirit.

In John 20:22, Jesus breathed on the Apostles and told them to "receive the Holy Spirit." In Acts 1:8, he said, "You shall receive power when the Holy Spirit has come upon you." That happened at Pentecost.

Like God, when we speak, the only way our voice can make a word is by forcing air or breath to make the word an audible sound. This air also makes life by the blood flowing health to the heart and brain and all the organs. Scientists have looked at atoms and split the atom (quantum physics) and subatomic particles. They have recently found that the subatomic particle, the minutest dot, in itself originates as a low soft sound.

As born-again Christians, we now have the same power (the Holy Spirit) that raised Jesus from the dead, and this power is from God. Our DNA and blood are now supernaturally and spiritually the same as God's. Here are some examples of what Jesus said we can do: we can raise the dead to life, heal the sick, cast out demons or evil spirits, change wine into water, declare and decree life, healing, and wholeness for someone in another town or city, and it is a done deal in Jesus's name.

Psalm 82:6 says, "I said, you are gods, and all of you are sons of the Most High." John 10:34, 35 also says, "I said you are gods, to whom the word (breath) came." Since the Father, Son, and Holy Spirit is in me, I am just like them—perfect, pure, holy, blameless, and righteous. I declare just as Jesus said, "I only speak these things as the Father taught me. He who is of God hears the words of God."

The question that is now being asked is, why do bad things happen to good people? It's because good people make bad choices, and we have to pay the consequences for the bad choices that we make.

Affirmation

I now have the same power in me that raised Jesus from the dead, and nothing in the natural can touch my Spirit.

The Old Testament Symbolism to the New Testament

The Passover (blood)—is *substitution*: the lamb or thing that takes the place of another. (Salvation—Sozo) (Purpose—Power)

The Tabernacle (Jesus)—is *transmutation*: being baptized and born again; to change or alter in form or appearance to a higher nature. (Peace) (Provision—divine nature)

Pentecost (Holy Spirit)—is *transubstantiation*: the divine nature of God

The Eucharistic elements (communion) become the body and blood of Christ while still keeping only the appearances of bread and wine. (Promise–Holy of Holies)

8

Law and Grace

Abraham received grace through faith before the Law was given to Moses. The effects of the Law is life and death. No one could keep the whole Law, so the Law is called the ministry of death. "If we think that we are justified by the Law, we have fallen from grace" (2 Corinthians 3:7; Galatians 5:4).

The Law is void of the Holy Spirit. The Law to the Hebrews is called Torah. The Torah in Hebrew means to teach or instruct. This is the first (old) covenant. When we received grace without measure, it was from the new covenant, which comes through the blood of Jesus on the cross of love. This grace was given to us from God our Father as a gift.

Grace can never be earned. Jesus is the only channel to grace. John 1:17 says, "Jesus is grace and truth." The Law was not given to make you holy. If there is no Law, then sin is just sin, and there is no transgression. Transgression comes from the Law (Romans 4:15).

The grace of God began in the Garden of Eden after the fall of Adam and Eve. In Genesis 3:15, when God prophesied to Satan, he (Jesus) shall bruise you on the head and you shall bruise Him on the heel. This is called the covenant of the nail. In Romans 16:20, the Apostle Paul says, "And the God of peace will soon crush Satan under your feet. The grace of our Lord Jesus be with you." Revelation 12:17 says, "And the dragon

(Satan) was enraged with the woman, and went off to make war with the rest of her offspring, who keep the commandments of God and hold to the testimony of Jesus."

In Psalm 45:2, King David spoke of Jesus one thousand years before he was born. "Grace is poured upon Thy lips; therefore God has blessed Thee forever." Psalm 84:11, "The Lord gives grace and glory." Jesus is grace and truth.

If sin can stop grace from having an effect, then sin is greater than grace. Jesus's power, grace, and righteousness are greater than sin because of the blood. We are not called to examine one another; we are called to examine the lamb, who is Jesus, the final sacrifice for our sin. Let's use an example here: someone is guilty of adultery and murder. Does this stop God's grace and mercy from working on their behalf? No!

The Greek word for grace is *charis*. Strong's translation: grace is a divine influence upon the heart and its reflection in your life. It causes your spirit to become new and it can be seen in your life (Acts 11:22, 23).

God's name in Hebrew is YHWH, to be translated in Hebrew as *Yud Hei Vav Hei*, correctly pronounced as Yahweh, and translated into English would mean, "open hand of grace." The religious leaders of Israel think that saying God's name is too holy for man to say, so they call him Adonai, which means Lord.

God's title is Elohiym, and it is his divine nature. The name of God YHWH (Yahweh), is a plural verb, not a noun, and the plural part is the Godhead or the Trinity.

God says, "I am a verb, I am that I am, I will be who I will be. I am alive and ever moving." He is a continuous, unfinished action. For something to move from death to life, you must introduce something dynamic and unpredictable into the mix and then to something living and present tense. This is to move from law to grace. Grace goes far beyond forgiveness. It is triumphant living, total freedom, and no expectations of us from God.

Sin-consciousness comes from the Law. Romans 5:14 says, "Death reigned from Adam to Moses, but sin was not imputed to mankind until the Law came at Mt. Sinai." Romans 6:14 says, "For sin shall not be master over you, for you are not under the Law, but under grace." Romans 4:8 and 2 Corinthians 5:19 also say, "Blessed is the man whose sin's the Lord will not take into account." Romans 5:21 tells us, "Even more than sin, righteousness reigns in life." Under the Law, righteousness is earned. Our righteousness as born-again Christians is not earned; it is a free gift from God. This does not mean that we can justify our sin.

In Romans 3:27, the law of faith makes us righteous. We can do through faith what we could not do through self-effort. Abraham believed God and was declared by God as being righteous by his faith.

Isaiah 54:14 says, "I am established, planted, and rooted in the righteousness of God in Christ. No oppression, no fear, nor terror, can come near me, and those that gather against me shall fall." Our God can handle Satan. Jesus stripped Satan of his ability and power in my life, and he's just a toothless lion with only a big roar.

Affirmation

Jesus made me whole and righteous by his shed blood on the cross of love, and I must continually be righteousness-conscious. No weapon formed against me shall prosper, and I'm not moved by circumstance or what I can see. I tell Satan to flee, and he has to flee.

"I am a letter of Christ written with the Spirit of God. Not on tablets of stone, but on the tablets of human hearts. But if the ministry of death, engraved on stone came with glory, how shall the ministry of the Spirit fail to be even more glorious?" (2 Corinthians 3:3, 7, 8). The devil knows that where there is a law, he'll use it against you. Stop being sin-conscious!

God has an ability that no man has. He can totally and completely forget things. God no longer has an issue with sin (Hebrews 8:12). He says, "I will remember your sins no more."

We need to just believe and receive what Jesus has already done over two thousand years ago on the cross of love. He said, "It is finished," so sit down and rest (have peace). Romans 1:15, 17 says, "Our requirement is the obedience of faith, which produces righteousness." This is the new covenant—to believe in Jesus. He emphasized and continuously said in the scriptures, "Do you believe?" In Jesus Christ, God has given us all things pertaining to life and happiness here on earth.

How to Receive Grace

1. Renew your mind (Romans 12:2). Cleanse your conscience (Hebrews 9:14). When you change (renew) your thinking, you will change your attitude, and then you will change your behavior.
2. Love gives you the access to the power and the anointing, and the anointing is faith. Love is not a feeling; it is a decision you make.
3. Say what you believe and be bold in a loving attitude.
4. See righteousness as a magnet to draw everything you need.
5. Don't have a guilt of non-imputed sin in your life. Stop beating yourself up.

Isaiah 54:17 says, "Righteousness is my vindication from the Lord God. I am established in righteousness." Faith establishes us in righteousness, and once it is truly established, there is no wavering, or even missing the mark won't keep you from it. "Receive your abundance of grace and the gift of righteousness in Jesus Christ our Lord" (Romans 5:17). This gift of righteousness is true grace.

The key in a Christian's life is to maintain your righteousness. Stop struggling to get what you already have. You cannot sin away this gift of righteousness. Did your good deeds change your status as a sinner before you were born again? No! So how can sin change your status as a Christian now?

Trust God and do good!

Romans 2:4 says the realization of the goodness and great love of God produces the repentance, salvation, and change in sinners. Grace is not an excuse to not be what God wants you to be. Love replaces the law, and it fulfills the law when God's love is in our hearts. You can sin and still be under grace. You receive grace after you get the power.

Love is the power!

Love = mercy and grace, which produces hope and faith, which imputes to us righteousness, truth, and peace (rest).

9

The Kingdom of God

The kingdom of God is governed by spiritual laws.

"Now then, if you will indeed obey My voice and keep My Covenant, then you shall be My own possession among all the people, for all the earth is Mine; and you shall be to Me a kingdom of priests and a holy nation" (Exodus 19:5, 6).

"They throne oh, God, is forever and ever; a scepter of uprightness is the scepter of Thy Kingdom" (Psalm 45:6).

"Thy kingdom is an everlasting kingdom, and Thy dominion endures throughout all generations" (Psalm 145:13).

"And in the days of those kings, the God of heaven will set up a kingdom which will never be destroyed, and that kingdom will not be left for another people; it will crush and put an end to all these kingdoms, but it will itself endure forever" (Daniel 2:44).

"Turn from your sin's and turn to God, because the Kingdom of Heaven is near" (Matthew 3:2). The kingdom of God was never meant to assimilate with man's culture.

Matthew 3:12 tells us that in those days, John the Baptist came preaching in the wilderness of Judea, saying, "Repent, for the kingdom of heaven is at hand." He was proclaiming the coming of Jesus Christ, the Messiah.

"Blessed are the poor in spirit for theirs is the kingdom of heaven. Blessed are those who have been persecuted for the sake of righteousness, for theirs is the kingdom of heaven…Thy kingdom come, Thy will be done, on earth as it is in heaven. For Thine is the kingdom, and the power, and the glory forever… But first, seek His kingdom and His righteousness; and all these things shall be added to you" (Matthew 5:3, 6:10, 13, 33).

"And I tell you this, that many (non - Jews) will come from all over the world and sit down with Abraham, Isaac, and Jacob at the feast in the Kingdom of Heaven" (Matthew 8:11).

"As you go to the lost sheep of Israel, preach, saying, the kingdom of heaven is at hand. To you, it has been granted to know the mysteries of the kingdom of heaven, but to them it has not been granted. The kingdom of heaven is like leaven, which a woman took, and hid in three pecks of meal, until it was leavened" (Matthew 10:7, 13:11, 33).

"But, if I cast out demons by the Spirit of God, then the Kingdom of God has come upon you" (Matthew 12:28).

"For the good seed, these are son's of the kingdom" (Matthew 13:38). "I will give you the keys of the kingdom of heaven; and whatever you bind on earth shall be bound in heaven; and whatever you shall loose on earth, shall be loosed in heaven" (Matthew 16:19, 18:18).

"Jesus breathed on them and said to them, 'Receive the Holy Spirit. If you forgive the sins of any, their sins have been forgiven them; if you retain the sins of any, they have been retained'" (John 20:22, 23).

"Let the children alone, and do not hinder them from coming to Me; for the kingdom belongs to such as these. Truly I say to you, it is hard for a rich man to enter the kingdom of heaven. It is easier for a camel to go through the eye of a needle, than for a rich man to enter the Kingdom of God" (Matthew 19:14, 23, 24).

"Truly, truly, I say to you, unless one is born-again, he cannot see the kingdom of God. Unless one is born of the water and the Spirit, he cannot enter into the kingdom of God. That which is born of the Spirit is Spirit" (John 3:3, 5, 6).

"For the kingdom of God is not eating and drinking, but righteousness, peace, and joy in the Holy Spirit" (Romans 14:17).

"But each in his own order; Christ the first fruits, after that, those who are Christ's at His coming. Then comes the end, when He delivers up the kingdom to the God and Father, when He has abolished all rule and all authority and power" (1 Corinthians 15:23, 24).

"For He (God) delivered us from the domain of darkness, and transferred us to the kingdom of His beloved Son" (Colossians 1:13).

"Therefore, since we receive a kingdom which cannot be shaken, let us show gratitude, by which we offer to God an acceptable service, with reverence and awe" (Hebrews 12:28).

"Listen, my beloved brethren; did not God choose the poor of this world to be rich in faith and heirs of the kingdom which He promised to those who love Him?" (James 2:5).

Affirmation

The authority and power are one. The reality is that the kingdom is already within us. We come from heaven, and we are to walk as Christ on the earth. The kingdom of God is his Son Jesus, the Holy Spirit, and his love in us and for us.

10

The Kingdom of Power

Your faith must be established, and you will be strong. No matter what happens, you will be firm.

"And these signs and attesting miracles will accompany those who have believed; in My name they will cast out demons, they will speak with new tongues; they will pick up serpents, and if they drink any deadly poison, it shall not hurt them; they will lay hands on the sick, and they will recover" (Mark 16:18, 19).

"All authority has been given to Me in heaven and on earth. Go therefore and make disciples of all nations (people), baptizing them in the name of the Father and the Son and the Holy Spirit, teaching them to observe all that I have commanded you; lo, I am with you always, even to the end of the age" (Matthew 28:18–20). Angels don't preach the Gospel. That authority has been given to mankind.

"And as you go, preach, saying, "the Kingdom of heaven is at hand. Heal the sick, raise the dead, cleanse the lepers, cast out demons; freely you have received, freely give" (Matthew 10:7, 8).

"Behold, I have given you authority to tread upon serpents and scorpions, and over all the power of the enemy, and nothing shall injure you. Nevertheless, do not rejoice in this, that the spirit's are subject to you, but rejoice that your names are recorded in heaven" (Luke 10:19, 20).

"*You shall receive power* when the Holy Spirit has come upon you; and you shall be My witnesses both in Jerusalem, and in all Judea and Samaria, and even to the remotest part of the earth" (Acts 1:8).

"Now to Him (God) who is able to do exceeding abundantly beyond all that we ask or think, according to the *power that works within us*" (Ephesians 3:20). This power came upon 120 disciples of Jesus Christ at Pentecost, which was about fifty days after Passover when Jesus was crucified on the cross of love.

"For we are not fighting against people made of flesh and blood, but against the evil rulers and authorities of the unseen (spiritual) world, against those mighty powers of darkness who rule this world and against wicked spirits in the heavenly realms" (Ephesians 6:12).

"The one who practices sin is of the Devil; for the Devil has sinned from the beginning. The Son of God appeared for this purpose, that He might destroy the works of the Devil" (1 John 3:8).

The Word of the cross is power. God's Word is truth, and truth is life.

"For the Word of the Cross is to those who are perishing foolishness, but to us who are being saved, it is the power of God" (1 Corinthians 1:18).

"We are human; but we don't wage war with human plans and method. We use God's mighty weapons, not mere worldly weapons to knock down the Devil's strongholds. With these weapons we conquer their rebellious ideas, and we teach them to obey Christ. The trouble with you is that you make your decisions on the basis of appearance" (2 Corinthians 10:3–7).

"And He (Jesus) is the radiance of His (God's) glory and the exact representation of His (God) nature, and upholds all things by the word of His (Jesus) power. When He (Jesus) made purification of sins, He sat down at the right hand of the Majesty on high; having become as much better than the angels, as He has inherited a more excellent name than they" (Hebrews 1:3, 4).

The church has put the faith of the "now" into the future. "Now faith is." We have been westernized in the name of civilization, and religion has devalued our faith. Why are miracles not happening in the church and there isn't any movement of the supernatural? Why do believers not have the power of God?

1. The church is full of optimism and hope, and there is a lack of expectation. We have confused faith with trust. Trust is a feeling that operates in relationships. We think that optimism is faith. It is not!

2. Skepticism is used to cover the lack of faith by discernment. People use discernment as a reason to reject supernatural faith and accept something that is false. The things of the Spirit scare people. That's why we don't speak in tongues and move in the Spirit anymore. We don't cast out demons anymore, and we call these false in the name of discernment. This is why faith is no longer working.

3. The church is using education as reality. Since when did you understand the works of God? Your faith must bring it into existence. The church today thinks that it is an organization, but it is actually an organism.

4. Christian faith has been formalized to the point that it no longer builds up. Preachers are speaking in the realm of reason and not to the Spirit. People have more reasons to say why something is impossible than reasons to say why it is possible.

5. Religion controls the church through traditions. Christianity is not a religion, and yet we have turned it into one. The church began as an organism, not an organization. Tradition and religion are from the past, and they have aborted the God of the now. They

have a God of the past and of the future but not a God of the now. When your faith is in the now, you must see the blind healed, the lepers cleansed, and the dead raised to life. Faith is now. The deaf must hear, the lame must walk, and the sinners must be transformed.

An organization is a functional administrational structure based on total conformity to its standards and rules. When the church began, it was a living organism that administered the power of God.

"You are truly My disciples if you keep obeying My teachings. And you will know the truth and the truth will set you free. I assure you that everyone who sins is a slave of sin. A slave is not a permanent member of the family, but a son is part of the family forever. So if the Son sets you free you will indeed be free" (John 8:32–36).

When you were born again, God gave you a measure of faith that you might move in the supernatural. Then religion got into your mind, and your mind deactivated the faith and indoctrinated it according to the denomination. The church has taught you to tolerate pain and demons rather than to cast them out.

The church is a living supernatural organism. You can do the expected. You can do the exceptional, and God does the extraordinary.

The opinions, wisdoms, traditions, knowledge, or religions of men have never established their faith in the Word of God. That is why the church has developed into an unbelief, and unbelief has now become our reality and is sin.

Ask any person why God cannot do miracles today. They will give you twenty reasons why God can't, and they will never say what he can do. This is why God hates unbelief, which is the legacy of the *fall*. Unbelief is a spirit that does not let you believe beyond your reasoning (five senses).

When God gave you faith, he gave the perspective of heaven. When we are born again in faith, we now see from God's perspective. The righteousness of God is revealed from faith to faith to faith, etc. Stop being stagnant and stuck. Now is your moment. Now.

Faith is not from the world or ourselves; it's from God.

11

The Life of Faith

Abraham believed God before the law came, and it was counted to him as righteousness by God, and God gave grace to Abraham before the law came. You must first believe in order to have the faith of God. Abraham had great belief and a little faith, and this faith was his obedience to God's Word.

Jesus told his apostles that they should have the faith of God. In Matthew 17:20, Jesus said, "I assure you, even if you had faith as small as a mustard seed you could say to this mountain, 'move from here to there,' and it would move. Nothing would be impossible." The thing about a mustard seed is that it is a very small seed, a little bigger than a grain of sand. The mustard seed is the only seed that cannot be genetically changed into something else. Like our faith should be, it will always remain a mustard seed.

"Love one another from the heart, for you have been born again not of seed which is perishable but imperishable, that is, through the living and abiding word of God" (1 Peter 1:22, 23). "The Word of God is a seed and the soil has no ability to say what the seed produces" (Luke 8:11). The seed makes a demand on the soil to give it life and growth. Just as the Word of God makes the demand to create and produce. The Bible says the Word of God is in your mouth and your heart. Jesus said, "You shall have whatever you say."

"The Law is not of faith. The Law is works, but faith must be born into our spirit" (Galatians 3:2, 7).

If God gives you the gift of righteousness by faith and blesses you, how can he not bless you the next time you screw up? And if this is not true, then the promise and the gift of righteousness is not true. Healing comes when you know you are righteous. Your righteousness is irreversible. You must take your eyes off the law.

Believing is faith. "For if those who are of the Law are heirs, faith is made void and the Promise is nullified. For this reason it is by faith, that in accordance with grace, in order that the Promise may be certain to all the descendants, not only to those who are of the Law, but also to those who are of the faith of Abraham, who is the father of all" (Romans 4:14–21).

Faith comes out of rest (peace).

"For the one who has entered His (God's) rest has himself also rested from his works, as God did from His. Let us therefore be diligent to enter that rest, lest anyone fall through the example of disobedience" (Hebrews 4:10, 11).

"For whatever is not of faith is sin. Without faith man cannot please God" (Hebrews 11:6). As Christians, even if you do sin, you can actually fall into grace. Sin cannot stop God's grace, and the goodness of God leads sinners to repentance. "Since faith has come, we no longer need the Law, the righteous shall live by faith" (Galatians 3:11, 20–27, 5:3–6).

In Luke 17:5–10, Jesus told us that faith is our servant, and this faith will eventually obey you. God has loaned you a servant, faith—name it and claim it/blab it and grab it. Romans 3:27 is the law of faith. Don't believe with your five senses. Tell yourself, "I'm gonna believe contrary to what my senses tell me. I will believe with my spirit." Wrong thinking will produce wrong belief.

"Truly, I say to you, whoever says to this mountain, 'Be taken up and cast into the sea, and does not doubt in his heart, but believes that what he says is going to happen, it shall be granted to him. Therefore, I say to you, all things for which you pray and ask, believe that you have received them, and they shall be granted to you'" (Mark 11:23, 24). If you don't know the will of God, you can't pray the prayer of faith.

Real faith doesn't deny the existence of a problem; it just denies the influence of the problem.

Jesus was using the mountain metaphorically. Metaphorically speaking, the mountain could be a problem in your life, a disease, or financial and material things you need.

Faith is now and works in the eternal. Faith by itself does nothing. You have to act on it. Faith is a positive response to what God has already done through his Word. Faith is your servant, so use it, and you can also have your faith working on more than one thing at a time.

True seed faith is, "Be it done unto me according to your word, O Lord." The word gives you the ability to do the impossible. Faith is a rest, and we who have believed have entered the Lord's rest, and now there is healing, forgiveness, wealth, prosperity, etc. "It is finished."

The only time you experience the Holy Spirit is when you walk by faith, and when I am really in faith, I don't possess it; it possesses me. Faith is looking within yourself and is the death of anxiety and the birth of total trust in God. Faith sees the invisible. "I believe because I have the gift of faith." Believing is seeing. Faith is only activated with love, and the greatest gift of all is love (see the diagram in "Cross of Love").

Intellect puts man on the throne. Faith puts God on the throne. The absence of faith brings denial, despair, and fear, and if you tolerate and accept fear in your life, you will cancel out faith. Faith operates in the here and now but lives in the there and then. Faith is a continuous attitude of believing until the answer is seen.

Faith receives by asking, and the principal part of faith is patience, and patience is power and grace. The law of righteousness is to love as Jesus loved, which will produce faith, power, and peace in our lives. Faith is the bridge from the spiritual realm into the physical or natural realm (Hebrews 11:1–3). Just because something is in an unseen realm doesn't mean it is nonexistent (Colossians 1:16; 2 Corinthians 4:18; John 1:14–17).

In 1 Peter 1:7–9, it says, "The proof of your faith, more precious than gold, which is perishable, even though tested by fire, may be found to result in praise and glory and honor at the revelation of Jesus Christ; and though you have not seen Him, you love Him, and though you do not see Him now, but believe in Him, you greatly rejoice with joy inexpressible and full of glory, obtaining the outcome as the outcome of your faith, the salvation of your souls."

You need to remove guilt and condemnation in your life in order for grace and righteousness to flow in your life. You can only release faith by speaking straight out of your mouth. Faith does not move mountains. Only faith inside your words moves a mountain in your life. Believe it, speak it, and it's done. God spoke the command, and it was.

James 2:14, 22–24 says godly faith without godly acts is not faith because faith is obedience. In verse 22, you see that his faith was cooperating with his works. A person can have incomplete faith because if you don't know what works or deeds are, you have incomplete faith. We also see that works and faith are partners.

The key to faith is patience. God promised Abram that he would have a son by his own seed when he was seventy-four years old. At the age of ninety-nine, God changed Abram's name to Abraham and Sarai to Sarah. The h or hei was added to their names, which is the fifth letter of the Hebrew alphabet (hei). Five is the number for grace. It was then that Sarah became pregnant at about the age of ninety. Abram believed God by faith, and God gave him grace. Abraham waited twenty-five years at ninety-nine years of age for the promise of his son, Isaac, from God.

12

The Gift of the Spirit

The Holy Spirit was in Adam and Eve at creation, but he left their spirit and departed from them at the fall in the Garden of Eden. This was the death that God spoke of when he said, "In the day that you eat of the fruit, you shall surely die." So today, in order for mankind to get back to God, we must become believers. Jesus said, "Unless you become born again (get the Holy Spirit back in you), you will not enter or see the kingdom of God" (John 3:3).

After the fall in the garden, God would only give or pour out his Holy Spirit to man, as they had faith and belief in him. Examples: Noah, Abraham, Moses, Joseph, David, Solomon, etc.

The Holy Spirit of the Trinity wanted to get back into humanity freely and by mankind's own free will and choice.

Jesus said in Matthew 7:11, "If you then, being evil, know how to give good gifts to your children, how much more shall your Father who is in heaven give what is good (Holy Spirit) to those who seek Him?" The good gift that Jesus is talking about here is all that comes to us when we receive the Holy Spirit as born-again believers and the baptism of the Holy Spirit.

The Holy Spirit is not to be conceived in terms of an emotional experience. He is not mysterious or weird. He is not a mystical influence that pervades one's being, nor is he a power like electricity, which we can use for our purposes. He is a divine person and power equal with the Father and the Son in power and dignity, and he is equally to be loved, worshiped, and obeyed.

There is a line of teaching that leaves the impression that the Holy Spirit is a luxury for a spiritually elite group of advanced Christians and that those who do not have certain experiences are second class citizens. But that is a misconception. Indeed, Jesus taught exactly the opposite: "Will a father give a snake for a fish, or a scorpion for an egg?" (Luke 11:11–13). "How much more will your Father in heaven give the Holy Spirit to those who ask Him?" (Matthew 7:9).

In Acts 19:2–6, the believers told Paul, "We have not heard that there is a Holy Spirit." After instructing them in the baptism of the Holy Spirit, Paul laid hands on them, and the Holy Spirit came on them. The Holy Spirit had already been given on the Day of Pentecost to the whole church, but the Ephesian elders had to believe that and appropriate the divine gift. That acknowledged lack accounted for their apparently anemic witness.

Be Filled with the Spirit

The command, to be filled with the Spirit (Ephesians 5:18), is not directed just to holy people or to an advanced stage of the Christian life any more than bread, fish, and eggs are reserved for adults and kept from children. The Holy Spirit's ministry is an indispensable and universal need at every stage of the disciple's life. Being filled with the Spirit is the indispensable minimum for a Christian life. God does not hold his children to the bare essentials of life, but he opens to us an inexhaustible reservoir of blessing. The Holy Spirit anoints (fills) us with the presence of our Father God.

The tense of the verb in Ephesians 5:18 gives the sense, "Let the Holy Spirit keep on filling you." This is a continuous action as foretold by the Lord: "If anyone is thirsty, let him come to Me and drink." "Whoever believes in Me" as the scriptures have said, "streams of living water will flow from him." By this he means the Spirit, whom those who believed in him were later to receive (John 7:37–39). What does it mean to be "filled" in this passage? We are not passive receptacles waiting for something to be poured into us. We are vibrant personalities capable of being controlled and guided by the Holy Spirit, and that is what the word means. "Don't be controlled by the spirit of wine, which produces disorder, but be controlled by the Holy Spirit." Bring your life under his control.

The Promise of Power

"You will receive power when the Holy Spirit comes on you; and you will be My witnesses in Jerusalem, and in all Judea and Samaria, and to the ends of the earth" (Acts 1:8). Two words for power: *exousia*, which means authority, and *dunamis*, which means ability, power, energy.

This *dunamis* power is where we get the word *dynamite* from, but it is not the dynamite itself; it is actually the explosion of the dynamite that is the real power. The Holy Spirit can be in this sense; at times, the explosiveness is like dynamite.

"The Holy Spirit, whom God has given to those who obey Him" (Acts 5:32). Now we have: a new consciousness of Christ's presence; A new likeness to Christ's character (2 Corinthians 3:18), being "transformed into his likeness" and "the mind of Christ"; a new presence and experience of Christ's power within us.

In John 16:7–9, Jesus said, "When He, the Holy Spirit, the Helper comes, He will convict the world of sin, righteousness, and judgment. Concerning sin, because they do not believe in Me." Once a sinner believes in Jesus as being the Son of God and their Lord and Savior in their heart, the Holy Spirit comes and lives in their spirit and soul. Now they are born again and become true sons and daughters of God our Father.

The purpose of the Holy Spirit is to glorify Jesus and to help us, comfort us, teach us, and show us the plans that God has for us (John 16:13, 14).

The Feast of the Passover in the Old Testament became the Lord's Supper or communion meal in the New Testament. This new covenant happened the night before Christ was crucified on the cross of love. The gift of the Holy Spirit's manifestation came to all the apostles, disciples, and believers in Jesus. There was 120 people in the upper room at Pentecost, which is fifty days after the feast of Passover. This event of the Holy Spirit coming upon the 120 people in the upper room at Pentecost is called the baptism of the Spirit.

To this day, whenever the Law of Moses is read to the Jews or those under the law, a veil lies over their hearts, but whenever a man comes to the Lord Jesus, the veil is taken away (2 Corinthians 3:15–18).

Now the Lord is the Spirit, and where the Spirit of the Lord is, there is liberty and freedom. But we all, with unveiled face beholding as in a mirror the glory of the Lord, are being transformed into the same image, from glory to glory to glory, just as from the Lord, the Spirit.

In Romans 8:26, 27, what is the Spirit doing? He is speaking in tongues, praying in tongues, and singing in tongues. The Holy Spirit goes to the Father and asks for us, and then He comes back to us and speaks to us of God's plan for us. The Holy Spirit wants to show us what is to come. When I am speaking in tongues, I am speaking out the perfect plan of my high priest, Jesus. It can't be just a word but a word in faith and prayer. Mark 11:24 says, "Believe and you'll receive, don't doubt."

"The promise, the Holy Spirit is unto you" (Acts 2:39). "But the fruit of the Spirit is love, joy, peace, patience, kindness, goodness, faithfulness, gentleness, self control; against these things there is no law" (Galatians 5:22).

"Build yourself up in faith by praying in the Holy Spirit" (Jude 1:20). When you pray in tongues, you're speaking the words of God. "The kingdom of God is not just a lot of talk, but is power, and it is the ability to get results" (1 Corinthians 4:20, 21). "Do you not know that your body is the temple of the Holy Spirit who is in you, whom you have from God, and that you are not your own?" (1 Corinthians 6:19). You have to start casting out devils yourself. Don't tolerate things that you have the power to overcome, which is everything seen and unseen.

"And Jesus whom God raised from the dead, did not undergo decay. Therefore let it be known to you brethren, that through Him, forgiveness of sin's is proclaimed to you, and through Him everyone who believes is freed from all things from which you, on your own, could not be freed, through the Law of Moses" (Acts 13:36–39).

Affirmation

The Holy Spirit is the gift of grace, the power is grace, the kingdom is in me. And it is the power in me to advance the kingdom. Pray for it, believe it, and it's a done deal. I am living by the power, overcoming by the power, and the kingdom of God is inside me.

13

The Unlimited Spirit of God

"And God breathed into Adam's nostril's the breath of life, and man became a living being (supernatural)" (Genesis 2:7).

Jesus said, "All power and authority has been given unto you" (Luke 24:49). "For John baptized with water, but you shall be baptized with the Holy Spirit not many days from now" (Acts 1:5, 8). "You shall receive power when the Holy Spirit has come upon you; and you shall be My witnesses even to the remotest parts of the earth."

The power and authority that Jesus has given to us at Pentecost is for the Holy Spirit of our Father, God, to come and live in us. Jesus stripped the devil of his power at the cross of love. The only power the devil (Satan) has today, we give to him.

As born-again Christians, our body and soul are the temple (dwelling place) of the Holy Spirit of God. Spirit must take on form to be effective in this time continuum dimension. We must look beyond the form (the physical) to spirit. There is no healing because people pray for the form and not the spirit. The warfare of the mind is between what you think and say, and the second battle is between what you say and what manifests from your words.

When our human form becomes inhabited by the Holy Spirit, now the form is spirit. We are now changed (metamorphosis) into a totally new creature or creation. Now we have a new spiritual form. The old form was man. First, the earthly and then the heavenly. First, the natural and then the supernatural, and the supernatural brings unlimited knowledge and power. The Holy Spirit is the full and unlimited power of Christ.

There are three baptisms: water, blood, and the Holy Spirit and fire. The first is the water, the second is the blood, and the third is the Holy Spirit, which is the power to command nature and destroy the works of the devil. An example of the third baptism is found in Genesis when God told Adam to take dominion and authority over all the earth. The third baptism is a divine nature attitude (DNA) that has no limitations.

In Matthew 3:11, John the Baptist said, "As for me, I baptize you with water for repentance, but He (Jesus) who is coming after me is mightier than I, and I am not fit to remove His sandals; He will baptize you with the Holy Spirit and fire."

Affirmation

I am not ruled by or living by the time continuum of this world. I am an eternal citizen of the heavenly realm of the Trinity. The past has passed, and the future hasn't happened yet. The now is all that matters in my life. The now is eternal. Eternity is not a time dimension; it is a nature. My power and authority comes from the Lord, the Holy Spirit, the giver of life, and I am plugged into Him. His power gives me life, strength, wisdom, knowledge, compassion, love, faith, and grace."

The new covenant prayer is to pray in Jesus's name. It is in his authority that you're praying, and you are praying as him.

Blasphemy of the Holy Spirit is denying the life of the Holy Spirit in the reality of Jesus's body or our body. Spirit responds to spirit, and flesh (mind and body) responds to flesh. Our gifting as Christians is the fruit of the presence of Christ in the Holy Spirit. Job 33:4 says, "The Spirit of God made me and the breath of the Almighty gives me life." In John 4:24, Jesus said, "God is Spirit and those who worship Him must worship in Spirit and truth."

In John 16:13, Jesus said, "He (the Holy Spirit) will not speak on His own initiative, whatever He hears, He will speak; He will disclose to you what is to come, He will glorify Me." "Those who are according to the flesh set their minds on the things of the flesh, but those who are according to the Spirit, the things of the Spirit. For the mind set on the flesh (I can do it myself, my own ability) is death, but the mind set on the Spirit is life (zoe) and peace" (Romans 8:5–17).

"However, you are not in the flesh, but in the Spirit, if indeed the Spirit of God dwells in you. But if anyone does not have the Spirit of Christ, he does not belong to Him. And if Christ is in you, though the body is dead because of sin, yet the spirit (human) is alive because of righteousness. But if the Spirit of Him (God) who raised Jesus from the dead dwells in you, He who raised Christ Jesus from the dead will also give life (zoe) to your mortal bodies through His Spirit who indwells you. For all who are being led by the Spirit of God, these are sons of God" (Romans 8: 9–14).

Verses 26 and 27 tell us, "He searches the heart (thoughts, reasonings, will, understanding, affections). He knows what we need before we even ask. He who searches the hearts knows what the mind of the Spirit is, because He intercedes for the saints (holy ones) according to God." "The Spirit searches all things, even the depths of God, and reveals it to us" (1 Corinthians 2:10). "We Christian's are a letter of Christ cared for with the Spirit of the living God on tablets of human heart's" (2 Corinthians 3:3–6, 17).

"It is the New Covenant of the Spirit that gives life. Now the Lord is the Spirit, and where the Lord is there is liberty (freedom)." Galatians 4:6 says, "The Spirit of God and His Son tells us we are son's." Galatians 5:5 also says, "For we through the Spirit, by faith, are waiting for the hope of righteousness."

"Blessed be the God and Father of our Lord Jesus Christ, who has blessed us with *every spiritual blessing in the heavenly places in Christ*, just as He chose us in Him (Jesus) before the foundation of the world, that *we should be holy and blameless before Him (God) in love*. He (God) predestined us to adoption as sons through Jesus Christ to Himself, according to the kind intention of His will" (Ephesians 1:3–5).

"Now having believed, you were sealed in Him (Jesus) with the Holy Spirit of promise, Who is given as a pledge of our inheritance. The unity of the Spirit in the bond of peace. One body, and one Spirit, one hope, one Lord, one faith, one baptism, and one Father of all" (Ephesians 1:13, 14/4:3, 4). Unity is oneness as it is also in the Trinity.

"But God, being rich in mercy (forgiveness) because of His great love with which He loved us, even when we were dead in our transgressions *made us alive together with Christ* and *raised us up with Him, and seated us with Him in the heavenly places, in Christ Jesus*" (Ephesians 2:4–6).

"God jealously desires the Spirit which He has made to dwell in us" (James 4:5). In 1 Peter 3:18, Christ has made us alive in the Spirit. In 1 John 3:23, 24, it says, "Believe in the name of His Son, Jesus Christ, and love one another. And we know this that He abides in us by His Spirit that He has given us" (also 1 John 4:13).

"Jesus came by the water and the blood, and it is the Spirit who bears witness because the Spirit is the truth. The three bear witness, the Spirit, the water, and the blood, and the three are in agreement" (1 John 5:6–8).

"I was in the Spirit on the Lord's day (Sunday, first day of the week)" (Revelation 1:10). The Spirit and the Bride say, "Come and let the one who is thirsty come; let the one who wishes, take the water of life without cost" (Revelation 22:17).

"The preaching of the word of God, that is, the mystery which has been hidden from the past ages and generations; but has now been manifested to His saints, the riches of the glory of this mystery among the Gentiles, which is Christ in you, the hope of glory. For you have died and your life is hidden with Christ in God. When Christ, who is our life, is revealed, when you also will be revealed with Him in glory. But Christ is all, and in all" (Colossians 1:25–27, 3:3, 4, 3:11).

No other religion in the world can claim what we Christians can: our God, Lord Jesus, and the Holy Spirit lives in us believers who are truly born again. Their Muhammad, Gautama Buddha, Confucius, Mohandas Gandhi, etc. does not live in their being.

Affirmation

I'm not waiting for the Holy Spirit to come; I brought the Holy Spirit with me. I am in him, I have the mind of Christ, and he is not separate from me.

14

The Cross of Love

The God of love and grace took all his wrath and anger with mankind and put it all on his only begotten Son, Jesus Christ, who was sinless. It pleased God that his only begotten Son should die for all mankind, and he declared and was glad to proclaim his Son guilty instead of mankind. This is called substitution. God was not only the righteous judge but also the prosecutor and the jury. The ultimate, perfect, unblemished, and true lamb of God died in our place to eradicate sin from the world and to destroy the devil.

In John 14:6, Jesus said, "I am the Way, the Truth, and the Life, no one comes to the Father but by Me." There is only one way to heaven, and that's through the Cross of Jesus Christ. "The mystery kept secret for long ages past, but now is manifested" (Romans16:25, 26). "The mystery of godliness is that Jesus is God manifest in the flesh" (1 Timothy 3:16). "He (Jesus) existed in the form of God and He emptied Himself taking on the form of a bond-servant and was made in the likeness of men, He humbled Himself, by becoming obedient to the death on the cross" (Philippians 2:5–8).

The love of God brought Adam and Eve into the presence of God. Therefore, when they fell, they lost the knowledge of the presence of God. Their minds fell the farthest. We must be filled with nothing less than the life of God in order to be healed, forgiven, and made new. Jesus did not come to make bad men good; he came to make dead men live and to defeat the devil. Thus, stated simply, to have communion with God means to have a share in his divine life. "He lives in me and I in Him" (John 14:20; 2 Peter 1:2–4).

To know the personal God is to know God in the manner in which persons are known. The content of a person always has an infinite quality, and this is especially so of God. Thus, to know Christ is to know Him as Son, and hence Son of the Father. When it says that Adam knew his wife, the Greek word for this is *spermos*, as in intercourse. This is the same way that we are to know God and Jesus in the spiritual realm and also them knowing us. Love alone reveals the true shape of the universe.

Through his death on the cross of love and his resurrection, Jesus has satisfied the judgment and penalty of God for all of mankind's sin. Romans 6:23 says, "The wages of sin is death." The requirement was the penalty of death. We no longer have to pay this penalty of death because Jesus did it for us of his own free will and choice. God's love declares us not guilty of the original sin given to us genetically by Adam and Eve and says no more death penalty to humanity. If we think that when we sin now after being born again, that we deserve death, this is legally called double jeopardy. Jesus died for all sin past, present, and future. How many of your sins were in the future before you were born again? All of them, of course! How many of mankind's sins were in the future when Jesus died on the cross for all of them? All of them.

"Jesus entered the holy place, having obtained eternal redemption (life), and we have obtained an eternal inheritance" (Hebrews 9:12, 15). "We are sanctified (washed pure and clean, blameless) through the offering of the body of Jesus Christ once for all time" (Hebrews 10:10). We are free from the condemnation of sin past, present, and future. Our sins are forgiven before we commit them.

"We are of the general assembly and the church of the first-born who are enrolled in heaven, and to God, the Judge of all, and to the spirits of righteous men made perfect. You have come to Jesus, the one who mediates the new covenant between God and people, and the sprinkled blood, which graciously forgives instead of crying out for vengeance as the blood of Abel" (Hebrews 12:23).

We can't view God today in the eyes of the Old Testament. Jesus was the lightning rod that attracted all of God's wrath and anger. God can be just in his righteousness in order to satisfy his wrath to declare us righteous at the cross. Sin is no longer an issue with God anymore because it was totally eradicated on the cross of love. The result of the death on the cross is: God now says that we are all declared his righteousness through his precious and beautiful Son, Jesus.

True love is mercy, which means forgiveness. Mercy came from God before grace, and this is the character of God our Father. He determined in the beginning, in the book of Genesis, to first of all forgive mankind of their sin. God's love is true forgiveness (mercy), and this is truth and grace to the ultimate level. Since God is love and forgiveness, He says, "If you don't forgive others of their wrongs toward you, I'll not forgive you of your sin's and fault's" (Matthew 6:14, 15; Mark 11:25, 26).

Ultimate faith only works through love. God is love, and his goodness and mercy are pursuing you all the days of your life. Romans 5:1–11 says nothing works without love. Galatians 5: 6 also says faith only works through love. We need to gain access by faith into grace. This is the ability to gain admittance into God's power. Love moves through truth and grace by flowing into the pipeline of faith (Hebrews 11:6). Belief equals faith. The love of God satisfied the wrath of God through his Son, Jesus. The Lord God gives us free forgiveness, righteousness, and eternal life just by mankind having faith in Jesus.

This is a diagram of the Pipeline of Love and Faith. The beginning is:

Love →()→ → Grace →()→ Righteousness

Grace is the power (force). My belief taps into the pipeline of faith, which now gives me grace and righteousness.

We must believe God's Word in order to access his grace. Sin cannot stop God's grace in your life anymore. "For by grace you have been saved through faith; and that not of yourselves; it is the gift of God" (Ephesians 2:8). Grace that is not for the kingdom of God is called talent.

An example:

Love *gives*/Grace *supplies*/Faith *receives*
(sent–Son)/(Jesus died)/(believe and receive)

God's love is a love that protects, but it is also a love that prevents. The Lord may say no at times of pain and suffering in order to lead us to trust completely and totally in him. It can also be to humble us as he walks with us through the refining fires. This refining fire will make us pure and blameless. We must realize that his eternal love is not always a pampering love. The bottom line is, God's love is a holy perfecting love. God says that we are to be perfect and holy, just as he is perfect and holy. Listen to your heart and not your mind, will, emotions. Your heart is only about eighteen inches from your mind. Don't miss getting to heaven by eighteen inches.

My victory and blessings are only from the blood of Jesus, which is the cup of blessing and communion. "He (God) has given to us exceeding and great promises, and we are partakers of the divine nature of God" (2 Peter 1:3–4). And this is what I call DNA (Divine Nature Attitude).

"The word of grace is truth and love" (Acts 14:3). "The testimony unto the word of His grace" (Acts 20:32). "He is upholding all things by the word of His power" (Hebrews 1:3).

The world says that death is final, but the Lord says love is final. Jesus died on the cross of love, but on the third day, love raised him back to life. You receive a crown for life when you love, and when you love God, you always win (Romans 8:28).

In Genesis 1:26, God said, "Let Us make man in Our image, after Our likeness." God is Spirit, therefore, mankind who is similar to God possesses an immortal eternal spirit. We humans resemble God in certain aspects without being equal to God. And being like God, mankind has the capacity with the power to think, feel, and decide for moral choice and spiritual growth or decline.

Since the fall of Adam and Eve, mankind is no longer in the perfect state of innocence as at that time and no longer has godlike attributes. Since that time to now, mankind has the sin genetic makeup of Adam and Eve. When they no longer trusted or believed God, they became sin-conscious. The Bible calls this generational curses or sins. Sin brings death, decay, disease, and sickness. When Jesus died on the cross of love, he died to take all sins, disease, sickness, and curses away. God has thrown them all into the sea of forgetfulness. He remembers them no more.

"It was the Father's good pleasure for all the fullness to dwell in Him, and through Him to reconcile all things to Himself, having made peace through the blood of His Cross" (Colossians 1:19–22).

By Christ's atonement (death) for our sins, we now have reached attainment. We have attained righteousness. Before his death on the cross, Jesus told his disciples, "Deny yourself, take up your cross daily, and follow me." This means to die to your own wants, needs, desires, and agendas.

The night before Jesus was crucified on the cross, he wanted to give us three very important things: peace, love, and joy. The first thing he wanted to give us is *peace*. "I am leaving you with a gift—peace of mind and heart. And the peace I give isn't like the peace the world gives. So don't be troubled or afraid" (John 14:27). The second thing he left to us is *love*. "I have loved you even as the Father has loved me. Remain in My love. When you obey Me, you remain in My love, just as I obey My Father and remain in His love" (John 15:9). The third thing he left us is *joy*. "I have told you this so that you will be filled with My joy. Yes, your joy will overflow" (John 15:11).

We need to live our lives by being constantly conscious of Jesus and God's love for us. Jesus and God is love, and therefore, love died for us on the cross of love. We are his beloved, we are the bride of Christ. To love as Jesus loved, to the Christian, is to be perfect, and this is to fulfill the law of righteousness. We are to have no more consciousness of sin in our lives! "The blood of Jesus cleanses us from all sin" (1 John 1:7). (This is a present, active participation.) It is a continuous constant process. "We are a part of the church that does not have any spot or wrinkle" (Ephesians 5:25–30). (This is a present, perfect participle.)

Love is not mere blind affection but the creative will to do good. Knowing is growing, and love is the skin of knowing. Those who are in Christ are life-giving spirits. Prayer is exercising your divine authority as a Christian.

"The secret things belong to the Lord our God, but the things revealed belong to us and our son's forever. The images are now manifest to mankind, and the light which is in them, is hidden in the image of the light of the Father. He will manifest Himself, and His image is concealed by His light" (Deuteronomy 29:29).

Affirmations

God is love, and his only begotten Son is love. Jesus's blood is love. Love died on the cross of love for me. Jesus's blood is much more precious than gold or diamonds because it is the blood of God, His Father.

I found out that love is my responsibility and that in me is the way, the truth, and the life. I set the spiritual laws in motion by the words of my mouth, and if I am one with Christ, do I have to repent? Christ Jesus doesn't sin, and I am created in the exact image and likeness of God.

The love of God gives me the light, and I have come from the light. His love has originated through itself. I not only have the light; I will be the light. I am the light of the world.

My prayer of my love for my God:

My Father, it's just that the very thought of us so happy appears in my mind as a wonderful, beautiful, mysterious thing in my life. I have a legacy of love, and the greatest gift of love is to pray. I have prayed and asked God to seal my heart with his love. Jesus appearing in me is the kingdom come. The glory God desires is a daily relationship with each other in truth and love. Amen.

15

Life Comes Out of Death

Jesus was born to die for all true believers. In John 12:23, 24, Jesus said, "The hour has come for the Son of Man to be glorified." This meant that he was to die for our sins on the cross of love about five days later. "And the glory which Thou has given Me, Father, I have given to them that they may be one; just as We are one" (John 17:22).

"Amen, amen, I say to you unless a grain of wheat falls into the ground and dies, it remains by itself alone; but if it dies, it bears much fruit." Galatians 5:22, 23 says the fruit of the Spirit is love, joy, peace, patience, kindness, goodness, faithfulness, gentleness, self-control; against these there is no law (the fruit is in the root).

"And the Lord God made clothing for Adam and Eve from animal skins and hides" (Genesis 3:21). This was the first blood sacrifice to cover sin.

"In the beginning was the Word, the Word was God, in Him was life (*zoe*), and the life was the light of men" (John 1:4). "For just as the Father raises the dead and gives them life (*zoos*—alive), even so the Son also gives life (*zoe*) to whom He wishes" (John 5:21). *Zoe* in Greek is the life that is in God. (I believe this has been given to us as true believers since Jesus is in us by the Holy Spirit.)

Zoos life is to just be alive; *zoe* life is God's eternal life.

"He who hears My word and believes Him who sent Me, has eternal life, and does not come into judgment, but has passed out of death into life (*zoe*). For just as the Father has life in Himself, even so He gave to the Son to have life (*zoe*) in Himself; and He gave Him authority to execute judgment because He is the Son of Man" (John 5:24, 25, 27). (I believe that when Jesus comes to live in us by and in the Holy Spirit, we now have this same life (*zoe*) in ourselves to appropriate and give to others.)

"The Father loves the Son and has given all things into His hands. He who believes in the Son has eternal life, he who does not obey the Son, shall not see life, the wrath of God abides on him" (John 3:35, 36).

"I am the bread of life, and this is the bread that came down from heaven, so that one may eat of it and not die (eternally). I am the living bread that came down out of heaven; if any one eats of this bread he shall live forever; and the bread which I shall give for the life of the world is My flesh. Unless you eat the flesh of the Son of Man, and drink His blood, you have no life (*zoe*) in yourselves, for My flesh is true food, and My blood is true drink" (John 6:40–53).

"It is the Spirit who gives life (*zoe*), the flesh (body) profits nothing; the words that I have spoken to you are Spirit and are life (*zoe*)" (John 6:63).

God our Father and Jesus His Son do not see physical death of the body as an eternal death. They see it as only being asleep. Eternal death to them is the spiritual death, loss of the Holy Spirit, or never having the Holy Spirit in our life. The twelve-year-old daughter of Jairus who had died, the young man whose funeral procession had already begun, and Lazarus who was dead for four days and in the tomb already, in Jesus's thinking, were only sleeping. Jesus raised his dear friend, Lazarus, from the dead by the power of his word and the Holy Spirit. The word of his power and the Holy Spirit also raised the young man to life. Likewise with Jairus's little girl.

(Note: babies and children up to a point where they are held accountable by God for their beliefs and sins, when they die, they go directly to heaven.)

"For this reason the Father loves Me, because I lay down My life (soul) that I may take it again. No one has taken it away from Me, but I lay it down on My own initiative. I have authority to lay it down, and I have authority to take it up again. This commandment I received from the Father. I and the Father are one (unity)" (John 10:17,18, 30).

"I am the resurrection and the life (*zoe*), he who believes in Me shall live even if he dies, and everyone who lives and believes in Me shall never die" (John 11:25, 26).

The master key is love. "A new commandment I give to you, that you love one another, even as I have loved you, that you love one another" (John 13:34.) "In this is love; not that we loved God, but that He loved us and sent His Son to be payment (death) for our sin's. So, we ought to love one another" (1 John 4:10).

"Whatever you ask in My name, that will I do. If you ask anything in My name, I will do it" (John 14:13, 14). "If you abide in Me, and My words abide in you, ask whatever you wish, and it will be done for you" (John 15:7). "If you ask the Father for anything, He will give it to you in My name" (John 16:23).

"For this end, Christ died and lived again, that He might be Lord of both the dead and the living" (Romans 14:9). "I am the Aleph/Taw (the beginning and the end)" (Revelation 1:18).

"But now Christ has been raised from the dead, the 'first fruits' of those who are asleep (dead). For as in Adam all die, so also in Christ all shall be made alive" (1 Corinthians 15:20–22). Verse 36 says, "That which you sow does not come to life unless it dies." Verses 51 to 54 also tell us, "Behold, I tell a mystery; we shall not all sleep, but we shall all be changed, in a moment in the twinkling of an eye, at the last trumpet; for the trumpet will sound, and the dead will be raised imperishable, and we shall be changed. But when the perishable will have put on the imperishable, and this mortal will have put on immortality, then will come about the saying that is written, 'Death is swallowed up in victory.'"

"And this is eternal life, that they may know Thee, the only true God, and Jesus Christ whom Thou has sent. verse 17, Sanctify them in truth; Thy word is truth. verse 21, that they may be one; even as Thou Father, art in Me, and I in Thee, that they may be in Us; that the world may believe that Thou did send Me" (John 17:3). Verse 22 says, "And the glory which Thou has given Me, I have given them; that they may be one; just as We are one; I in them and Thou in Me, that they may be perfected in unity, Thou did love them, even as you did love Me."

16

The Body and the Blood

The power of the blood is only found in the value of the source, Jesus. The reason Jesus's blood was so precious was because it is the blood of God.

It is a medical and scientific fact that the father gives the blood to the conceived child in the womb. This is why a blood test will show who the father is. When a man impregnates a woman with his sperm in intercourse, this is a blood transfer into the womb, and it is life (*zoos*).

In the Hebrew language, the word for blood is *dam*. You can see the connection between this root masculine noun and other words in the Old Testament. The first man's name was Adam or Yahdam, which means God-man. Another Hebrew word is *damuwth*, a feminine noun that means likeness, image, reddish from the earth or ground. The word *dam* not only means blood but also means the juice from grapes and is also used for the word *money*.

The Bible says the life (*zoos*) of the flesh is in the blood. The life in Hebrew is *nephesh*, which means breath, air, wind. This air or breath is what gives our blood healthy properties and helps it to flow. Without blood, our body will die.

The Passover: (blood) is substitution; the lamb (a person or thing that takes the place of another)

The Tabernacle: (church) is transmutation; being baptized and born again (to change or alter in form or appearance to a higher nature)

Pentecost: (Holy Spirit) is transubstantiation; the divine nature of God; the Eucharist or communion elements become the body and blood of Christ while still keeping only the appearances of bread and wine.

In John 6:32–35, Jesus said, "It is not Moses who gave you the bread from heaven, but it is My Father who gives you the true bread out of heaven. For the bread of God is that which comes down out of heaven, and gives life (*zoe*) to the world…I am the bread of life, he who comes to Me shall not hunger, and he who believes in Me shall never die."

"This is the bread which comes down out of heaven, so that one may eat of it and not die. I am the living bread that came down out of heaven; if anyone eats of this bread, he shall live forever; and the bread also which I shall give for the life of the world is My flesh…Truly, truly, I say to you, unless you eat the flesh of the Son of Man and drink His blood, you have no life in yourselves. He who eats My flesh and drinks My blood has eternal life, and I will raise him up on the last day. For My flesh is true food, and My blood is true drink. He who eats My flesh and drinks My blood abides in Me and I in him" (this is called transubstantiation)…As the living Father sent Me, and I live because of the Father, so, he who eats Me, he shall live because of Me…It is the Spirit who gives life; the flesh profits nothing; the words that I have spoken to you are Spirit and life" (John 6:50–63).

"Since then, the children share in the flesh and blood, He Himself likewise also partook of the same, that through death, He might render powerless, him who had the power of death, that is the devil; and might deliver those who through fear of death were subject to slavery all their lives. For assuredly, He does not give help to angels, but He gives help to the seed or descendants of Abraham (this is you and me)" (Hebrews 2:14–16).

Eucharist or communion means thanksgiving. We are to be thankful that God sent his Son Jesus to deliver us, and to take into his body disease, sickness, pain, and death for us. The Eucharist or communion is to partake of and become the divine nature of God and Jesus. When we partake of this, we are partaking in eternal life.

Baptism is to us Christians what circumcision was to the Hebrews (Jews). In 1 Corinthians 10:1–4, 16, 17, it is said that all the Jews were baptized into Moses in the cloud (the Holy Spirit), and all ate the same spiritual food, and all drank the drink from the spiritual rock (fire) that followed them, and the rock was Christ.

Is not the cup of blessing which we bless today a sharing in the blood of Christ? Is not the bread which we break a sharing in the body of Christ? Since there is one bread, we who are many, are one body, for we all partake of the one bread. This is true community and unity in the body of Christ. Jesus did not start a Christian denomination; he started the church as being the body of Christ.

We must be Jesus's body on earth, and his bread manifest in us, his body. The bread was not a type or symbol of Christ as many Christian churches are wrongly preaching and teaching. It was and still is Jesus's flesh. In Luke 22:19, 20, Jesus said, "This *is* my body and the new covenant *in* my blood."

The Blood of Love

When the Ebola virus broke out two years ago in Northern Africa, an American doctor contracted it. An antibody is a protein that surrounds the cells and stops the cancer or infection from growing, and it is a memory cell that carries the memory of how to overcome the specified virus. He was given the Z-Mat antivirus serum, and they only had enough for one person. He recovered and eventually no longer had the virus in his system. An NBC cameraman later contracted the virus, but they didn't have any more serum. So they took some blood from the cured doctor and injected it into him, and he was also healed. Jesus's shed blood works in this same way.

Jesus's blood carries the antibody of how he defeated sin—chokes it and kills it; death gives life. The blood of Jesus is liquid love, and it has the power to remove your sin from the memory of God. In Luke 22:20, Jesus said, "This cup which is poured out for you is the new covenant in My blood." You just need the faith in the blood of Jesus and its work in you. As said in 1 Peter 1:18, 19, you were redeemed (*sozo*, made whole) with the precious blood of Christ—pure and holy.

There is no effective weapon against the works of the devil except the blood of Jesus. In 1 Peter 1:2, it talks about the sanctifying work of the Spirit, that you may obey Jesus Christ and be sprinkled with his blood. Romans 3:23–24 says Jesus is the designation not only as the place where the sinner deposits his sin but that he himself is the means of expiation. This is done only through faith.

L' heiym (to life)—*mayim heiym* (living water)—*hei* (grace) in Hebrew and in the Greek *haima*. The blood of Jesus is still speaking in heaven. It flows from the heart of God our Father. Where the blood of Jesus flows, there the Holy Spirit goes. Revelation 1:5 tells us Jesus is the firstborn of the dead—to him who loves us and released us from our sins by his blood.

The Christian church began in the book of the Acts at Pentecost. In the early church, they didn't consider anyone added to the church until they were baptized. We are baptized when we hear the Word and believe in Jesus as the Son of God. There was no such thing as altar calls in the book of Acts. Those who heard and believed were then baptized. Everyone should be welcome to receive the communion (Eucharist). "They continued with one accord and breaking bread from house to house." The Jews didn't have a problem with rituals. You do because you are a secular (worldly) person.

Literally, when we eat our food, our body breaks down that food to be a substance that gives life to our body. There is not only a spiritual presence of Jesus in the bread and wine but also his physical presence. And the more you partake, the more you will become exactly like him. Jesus said, "I am the bread that came down from heaven. Why don't you believe me?"

Our motivation is our presence. We are to be Jesus's presence on the earth. You become his presence when you die to self—death to your own agendas, needs, wants, and rights, to do the will of God.

One of the reasons the Romans persecuted the early church, according to the documents from the governor of Jerusalem to Rome, is that "they (Christians) do strange rituals in the night, and even cannibalism." They thought the Christians were literally eating flesh and drinking human blood.

At some point, before, during, or after we partake of the bread and wine, it does become supernaturally Christ's body and blood. It is still bread and wine, but this is a supernatural mystery in the church. A Christian through faith only confessed that it was Jesus's body and blood.

The Apostle Paul said, "Many are sick and die because they take the communion as just mere bread and wine, and not as medicine for healing." Jesus's body, which was beaten and bruised for us, is for our healing today, and His shed blood for us is for our salvation.

Be glad that Jesus died for you. It's not how much you love him, but it's about how great a love he has for you. Rejoice that your name is now written in the Lamb's Book of Life in heaven. Your sins are no longer recorded or remembered by God.

When Jesus talks about being born again, he is making reference not only to us being awakened to our eternal purpose, unity, or community but to himself being reproduced in us also. This is called the great exchange. Jesus said, "Unless a grain of wheat falls to the ground and dies, it cannot multiply (reproduce), to give birth." His death and resurrection has made us to be God's final word to Satan and the world.

Our warfare is not with flesh and blood or demons that are attacking us. It's the thoughts in our mind that tell us as Christians that we are separate from Jesus and God.

Quit walking with God and start walking as God on this earth. We're not just mere humans; we are now a new creation. We are bone of his bone and flesh of his flesh. Jesus's death and resurrection has made us by our faith (belief), righteous by God our Father. The righteousness we receive is faith, truth, and grace, the unlimited power and favor of God in our lives.

The Bible says that our righteousness in Christ is a vindication from God.

17

Rest, It Is Finished

In five days (possibly five thousand years, for a day is a thousand years to the Lord), God had to make everything perfect, livable, and prepared for mankind and to get all of creation suitable for mankind to just rest and live happily as his beloved children. God provided everything that Adam and Eve needed for their existence here on earth (Genesis 1).

And by the seventh day, God completed his work which he had done—"It is finished"—and he rested on the seventh day from all his work that he had done. Then God blessed the seventh day and sanctified it to be purified, clean, and holy (Genesis 2:1–3).

Rest is Holy Spirit-directed activity. Rest means to have peace. The narrow way is a rest. God didn't have to rest. He doesn't get tired. He was just finished with his work. He wants us to rest. In the high priestly prayer of John 17:4, Jesus prayed to the Father, "I have glorified You on earth, having accomplished (finished) the work which You have given Me to do."

You have received salvation by what Christ has already done on the cross of love. Just before he breathed his last, Jesus said, "It is finished." So at the cross, we have now entered his rest. "For we who have believed have entered His rest. Let us therefore labor, work, and be diligent to enter that rest" (Hebrews 4:3–11). God designed mankind to operate out of rest and not stress, worry, fear, or anxiety. We dwell in the secret place of the Most High, and Satan cannot find or enter this secret place.

In the Garden of Eden, God said, "It is finished." In the Garden of Gethsemane, Jesus said, "I have finished your work, Father." We need to walk in the finished work of our Lord and God. Fear and worry stop God's release in your life. The devil cannot enter your rest.

"Therefore having been justified by faith, we have peace with God through our Lord Jesus Christ, through whom also we have obtained our introduction by faith into this grace in which we stand; and we exult in hope of the glory of God" (Romans 5:1, 2).

"But now in Christ Jesus you who formerly were far off have been brought near by the blood of Christ. For He Himself is our peace, who made both groups into one (Jew and Gentile) and broke down the barrier of the dividing wall, by abolishing in His flesh the enmity, which is the Law of commandments contained in ordinances, that in Himself He might make the two into on new man, thus establishing peace" (Ephesians 2:13–15).

The devil gets a foothold in your life when you speak fear, worry, anxiety, or negative words. Bad things happened to Job when he worried about his children. These all begin in your mind. The renewing of our mind is taking on the mind of Christ, which is a divine son-ship, and Jesus in us is the kingdom come. His being born and appearing in this world was not to bring the kingdom only; it was to conclude the kingdom of God—"It is finished."

Having the mind of Christ is direction without any doubt, and then grace flows in the worry-free areas of your life. The greatest thing for your family is for you to be carefree, happy, and joyful. God's people must have a throne attitude. Rest! Sit down until the problem is resolved.

The devil loves to have the old human nature to reign in the church. In the temple, the priests could never sit down.

Only the high priest sat down. Jesus our high priest has sat down at the right hand of the Father in heaven. Thus, we are to now sit down with them, be at peace, be still, and God will make our enemies our footstool.

In Hebrews 3:7–11, ten times the people didn't believe God, and he said, "I swore in My wrath, they shall not enter My rest." Isaiah 48:22 says, "There is no peace or rest for the wicked," says the Lord.

People still see healing as a work. Jesus's greatest miracles were done on the Sabbath day of rest, the seventh day. He told a man who was crippled from birth for twenty-eight years, "Rise up, take up your bed, and walk." The bed is a picture of rest. Hebrews 4:10, 11 says we are to labor and work to enter God's rest. God works better when people get out of the way. The greatest expression of faith in God is to rest.

God still performs miracles today, and even on the seventh day, Sabbath rest.

18

Will There Be a Rapture of the Church?

Rapture: a state or experience of being carried away by overwhelming emotion, a mystical experience in which the spirit is exalted to a knowledge of divine things, a manifestation of ecstasy or passion (*Webster's Dictionary*).

God is raising up a remaining generation, not an escape generation. Escapism from anything cannot prosper. The day is coming when the righteous will control.

In 1830, Margaret McDonald had a dream of the saints rising up to heaven in the air. Edward Ingram, her pastor, preached this dream as biblical doctrine. Scoffield expanded on this and called it rapture. The Dispensationalists have adopted this idea as one of their main doctrines of belief. This nonbiblical idea is now called the pretribulation rapture of the church.

Protestant denominations, Baptists, Methodists, Episcopalians, Pentecostals, Assemblies of God, and non-denominations have all bought into this theology of a pretribulation rapture, and they are today preaching and teaching this.

Escape rapture theology is at war with the divine nature of God's people. The Bible says that when we the saints (believers) die, our body remains and decays, and our Spirit returns to heaven and the Father.

In Matthew 3:2, 4:17 and Mark 1:5, Jesus said, "The kingdom of heaven is within you and at hand, here and now." The kingdom of God and heaven is not just a physical place but an unseen spiritual place. The kingdom of God is Jesus in me. In John 14:18, Jesus said, "I will not leave you as orphans. I will come to you." The generation that will remain (survive) is who Jesus is coming back for. If every believer is to be secretly raptured up into heaven, then why would Jesus need to come get his people, the church, to take them back to heaven?

The best reasoning that I can give to oppose a pretribulation rapture is this: the beloved apostles whom Jesus lived, ate, and slept with for three and a half years all died as martyrs terribly and horrifically. The only apostle that didn't get martyred was John the beloved, who died on the island of Patmos. Jesus was already in heaven with the Father, and the power of the Holy Spirit had already been given to all the believers. Jesus loved them all very much, so why didn't he have the power of God rapture them up into heaven before all the trials and tribulation came upon them? Why didn't God rapture into a cloud into heaven all the thousands of Christian men, women, and children who were fed to the lions and crucified?

"But when the Son of Man (Jesus) comes in His glory, and all the angels with Him, then He will set up His glorious throne. And all the nations will be gathered before Him' and He will separate them from one another, as the shepherd separates the sheep from the goats and He will put the sheep on His right, and the goats on His left" (Matthew 25:31–33). We are the sheep of his pasture. The goats are those that don't believe in Jesus.

In Luke 21:10–33, Jesus said,

Nations and kingdoms will proclaim war against each other. There will be great earthquakes, and there will be famines and epidemics in many lands, and there will be terrifying things and miraculous signs in the heavens. But before all this occurs, there will be a time of great persecution. You will be dragged into synagogues and prisons, and you will be accused before kings and governors of being My followers. This will be your opportunity to tell them about Me. So, don't worry about how to answer the charges against you. For I will give you the right words and such wisdom that none of your opponents will be able to reply.

Even those closest to you—your parents, brothers, relatives, and friends—will betray you. And some of you will be killed. And everyone will hate you because of your allegiance to Me. But not a hair on your head will perish! By standing firm, you will win your souls. And when you see Jerusalem surrounded by armies, then you will know that the time of its destruction has arrived. For those will be days of God's vengeance, and the prophetic words of the Scriptures will be fulfilled.

And there will be strange events in the skies - - - signs in the sun, moon, and stars. And down here on earth the nations will be in turmoil, perplexed by the roaring seas and strange tides. The courage of many people will falter because of the fearful fate they see coming upon the earth, because the stability of the very heavens will be broken up. Then everyone will see the Son of Man arrive on the clouds with power and great glory. So, when all these things begin to happen, stand straight and look up, for your salvation is near! Just so, when you see the events I've described taking place, you can be sure that the Kingdom of God is near! Heaven and earth will disappear, but My words will remain forever.

"So then, when the Lord Jesus spoke to them, He was received up into heaven, and sat down at the right hand of God" (Mark 16:19).

"He (Jesus) was lifted up while they were looking on, and a cloud received Him out of their sight. Two men in white clothing stood beside them; and they said, men of Galilee, why do you stand looking into the sky? This Jesus, who has been taken up from you into heaven, will come in just the same way as you have watched Him go into heaven" (Acts 1:9–11).

"For this we say to you by the word of the Lord, that we who are alive and remain until the coming of the Lord, shall not precede those who have fallen asleep. Then we who are alive and remain shall be 'caught up' together with them in the clouds to meet the Lord in the air, and thus we shall always be with the Lord" (1 Thessalonians 4:15–17).

If Jesus were to come back the second time for the rapture of the church and then take them home to heaven and then when he comes back to set up his millennial one-thousand-year reign in Jerusalem, this would then be a third coming. There is not three comings of Jesus in the Bible.

"When the Lord Jesus shall be revealed (in the Greek - Apokalupsis) from heaven with His mighty angels in flaming fire, dealing out retribution to those who do not know God and to those who do not obey the gospel of our Lord Jesus. And these will pay the penalty of eternal destruction, away from the presence of the Lord and from the glory of His power, when He comes to be glorified in His Saints in that day, and to be marveled at among all who have believed for our testimony to you was believed" (2 Thessalonians 1:7–10).

The word in the previous paragraph revealed, *Apokalupsis*, means revelation, uncovering, unveiling, disclosure. This grander and more comprehensive word includes not merely the thing shown and seen but the interpretation and the unveiling of the same, being separate points or moments therein. Christ's first coming was an epiphany and the second or *apokalupsis* will be more glorious.

"Now we request you, brethren, with regard to the coming of our Lord Jesus Christ, and our gathering together to Him. Let no one in any way deceive you, for it will not come unless the apostasy comes first, and the man of lawlessness is revealed, the son of destruction, who opposes and exalts himself above every so-called god or object of worship, so that he takes his seat in the temple of God, displaying himself as being God" (2 Thessalonians 2:1, 3, 4).

In Matthew 24:9, 22, 23, 37–39, Jesus said, "Then they will deliver you to tribulation, and will kill you, and you will be hated by all nations on account of My name…And unless those days had been cut short, no life would have been saved; but for the sake of the elect, those days shall be cut short… For the coming of the Son of Man will be just like the days of Noah, and they did not understand until the flood came and took them all away; so shall the coming of the Son of Man be."

"Then there shall be two men in the field, one will be taken (caught up), and one will be left (Noah). Two women will be grinding at the mill; one will be taken (caught up), and one will be left (Noah)" (Matthew 24:40, 41).

In Noah's day, before the flood, mankind was very evil. They were into their own selves; sexual immorality, homosexuality, entertainment and music were all people cared about, and they denied and didn't believe in God. Only one man was righteous in all the earth, and that was Noah.

Noah, his wife, and three sons with their wives were the only righteous who entered into the ark to be saved from the impending flood that was to cover the whole earth. The ark was a type or shadow of Christ. This is the relational covenant family of God, the ark. *Ark* also means casket or coffin, protection and safety.

My question to those who believe in a pretribulation rapture of the church is this: in the tribulation, during the time after the so-called rapture of the church, what happens to the people that are born again and saved? Why don't they then get immediately raptured to heaven to be with God, Jesus, and the saints?

The reason the church is broken today is because it is not relational. Many of us only care about our own fun, entertainment, pleasures, material things, and not others. "But the Spirit explicitly says, that in the later times, some will fall away from the faith, paying attention to deceitful spirit's and doctrines of demons by means of hypocrisy of liars" (1 Timothy 4:15).

Noah loved and cared for the people, and he preached to them about the coming disaster of the flood, but they disbelieved his words and mocked him. This same thing is happening very subtly in the church today.

The Dispensationalists say that the phrase "caught up" means rapture. Who was caught up, or taken away in the great flood? Not Noah and his family. It was the evil and the unbelieving worldly ones. We have the two examples that Jesus gives in the scriptures: "There were two men working in the fields, one was evil, the other righteous. The evil man was taken in death and the righteous man was left alive in the field. The second example is, two women grinding at the mill. One taken in death, the other left alive" (Matthew 24:40–44). These examples are exactly what Jesus was saying.

Verse 44 says, "Therefore, be on the alert, for you do not know which day your Lord (Jesus) is coming. For this reason, you be ready too; for the Son of Man is coming at an hour when you do not think He will." Jesus is saying here that we are to be the pure, blameless, and spotless bride that he is coming back for and not doing evil or ungodly things.

In 1 Thessalonians 4:13–18, it says Jesus is coming back in the clouds with the angels and those who already went to heaven called the saints. The dead in Christ will be given back new spiritual bodies and rise up to meet him in the air. Then we who are the saints alive on earth will also be changed into spiritual beings with no physical death and rise up with the others to meet Jesus in the air (lower or upper atmosphere).

Heaven in the Bible is described as being in three parts. The first heaven is the lower atmosphere of air we breathe, the second heaven is above the air atmosphere (universe), and the third heaven is where God dwells, and we can't see it with our physical eyes.

"We shall be with Jesus forever" (1 Thessalonians 4:17). In the New Testament, it does not—I repeat, does not—say that Jesus takes us all at that time to the third heaven where God dwells. We saints who have been glorified will go with him to Jerusalem, where he sets up his millennial thousand-year reign as Lord and King of heaven and earth. Those who are nonbelievers, unsaved sinners, who are alive when Jesus returns will still be alive on earth, and they are still subject to a physical death in this thousand-year period.

Jesus said in John 5:24, "Truly, truly, I say to you, he who hears My word, and believes Him who sent Me, has eternal life, and does not come into judgment, but has passed out of death into life." Romans 8:1 says, "There is, therefore, now, (today) no condemnation (judgment) for those who are in Christ Jesus." The unsaved sinners, those who denied or rejected Jesus as the Son of God, the antichrists, they will be judged according to their deeds or works for God. If their name was not found written in the Lamb's Book of Life, they were thrown into the lake of fire and brimstone for all eternity.

19

The Resurrection of Believers

There is not one church on earth and another in heaven. There is one church of which all Orthodox believers are members. In the God-man Christ Jesus, heaven and earth are united, and the distance between God and man of whatever sort is overcome.

One of the hallmarks of the two-story universe theory is its difficulty with the presence of God. God's presence is recognized as the source and gift of all life. The absence established by our culture is an effort to regulate the presence of God; now we want him, now we don't.

The resurrection of Christ is not an example of life after death but the destruction of death itself. The Christ who sits at the right hand of the Father is no ghostly spirit but the risen Lord who has carried earth and man to the right hand of the Almighty God. It is not a two-story account but the very basis for belief in a one-story universe.

Christ's resurrection is not the victory abstraction over reality but the victory of reality over the delusion of death and all its kingdom. It is the union of earth and heaven, created and uncreated. In such a union, there cannot be two metaphysical floors of reality.

The "great cloud of witnesses" is, in fact, the great company of heaven—the departed who are in the "hands of God." Their concerns are not separated from the body of Christ (the church).

Revelation says the concern of the inhabitants of heaven within the saints' vision is the matters on earth. The body of Christ is one body. There is only one church—not divided between those who have fallen asleep in Christ and those who remain behind.

My success or failure in my spiritual life is not my private business but the concern of a "great cloud of witnesses." They are not watching only as disinterested bystanders. They urge us and support us with their prayer. We are not alone. The "great cloud of witnesses" stands with me and in me in prayer.

In John 6:44, 47, Jesus said, "No one can come to Me unless the Father who sent Me, draws him; and I will raise him up on the last day." "Truly, truly, I say to you, he who believes in Me has eternal life." John 5:24 also says, "Truly, truly, I say to you, he who hears My word, and believes Him who sent Me, has eternal life, and does not come into judgment, but has passed out of death into life."

> That which you sow does not come to life unless it dies; and that which you sow, you do not sow the body which is to be, but a bare grain, perhaps of wheat or something else. But God gives it a body, just as He wished, and to each of the seed's a body of its own.

> All flesh is not the same flesh, but there is one flesh of men, and another of beasts, and another flesh of birds, and another of fish. There are heavenly bodies and earthly bodies, but the glory of the heavenly is one, and the glory of the earthly is another. There is one glory of the sun, and another glory of the moon, and another glory of the stars, for star differs from star in glory.

> So, also is the resurrection of the dead. It is sown (conceived) a perishable body, it is raised an

imperishable body; it is sown in weakness, it is raised up a Spiritual body. If there is a natural body, there is also a Spiritual body. So, it is written, "The first Adam became a living soul, the last Adam (Jesus) became a life giving Spirit." However, the Spiritual is not first, but the natural; then the Spiritual. The first man is from the earth, worldly; the second man is from heaven, Spiritual. And just as we have been born the image of the earthy, we shall bear the image of the heavenly.

Behold, I tell you a mystery; we shall not all sleep (die), but we all shall be changed, in a moment, in the twinkling of an eye, at the last trumpet; for the trumpet will sound and the dead shall be raised imperishable, and we all shall be changed. For this perishable must put on imperishable, and this mortal must put on immortality. When this happens, then will come about the saying that is written, "Death is swallowed up in victory. Oh, death, where is your victory? Oh, death, where is your sting?"

The sting of death is sin, and the power of sin is the Law, but thanks be to God, who gives us the victory through our Lord Jesus Christ. Therefore, my beloved brethren, be steadfast, immovable, always abounding in the work of the Lord, knowing that your toil is not in vain in the Lord. (1 Corinthians 15:35–58)

At the moment and time that Christ comes back to usher in the millennium, no sinner can, at that time, repent. So sad, but it's now too late.

Remember, we will be perfect, meaning we will be the soul that God had in mind all along. We will be like God, loving and unselfish as Jesus, and when like him, our one thought of delight is that God is, and is what he is, our all-loving Father.

One day soon, we will round a bend in the road, and our dreams will come true. We will live happily ever after. The long years in exile will be swept away in the joyful tears of our arrival home. Every day when we rise, we can tell ourselves, "My journey today will bring me closer to home. It may be just around the bend." All we long for, we shall have; all we long to be, we will be. All that has hurt us so deeply—the dragons and the nits, the arrows, and our false lovers, yes, and Satan himself—they will be swept away, and then eternal life begins. Amen (sealed in truth).

Affirmation

I'm not afraid of dying, the 666, the Antichrist, or the beast of Revelation. I am created to be higher in authority than the angels, and the devil is in submission to me.

Religious traditionalists have worshiped their own intellectual analyzation of what they think will happen. Psalm 37:22 says that "we shall inherit the earth and the wicked shall be destroyed." The elect are going to stay and be here on earth eternally with our Lord Jesus and Father God.

20

The Book of Life/The Lamb's Book of Life

I was reading about "The Lamb's Book of Life" in Revelation when the Holy Spirit spoke to me, and he said, "Go back to creation and see the truth about the Book of Life." All of a sudden, it came to me in my spirit—God created and made mankind in his image and likeness. He became a Father to us, and the Trinity was now mankind's parents. The Father walked and talked with his children, Adam and Eve, daily in the Garden of Eden until their fall.

Our Father God has recorded every birth from Adam and Eve until this very day in the Book of Life. A child at some period of time, possibly in their teenage years, will become responsible for their own beliefs, decisions, and actions in their lives. They will either accept or reject Jesus as their Lord and savior in their heart. When they accept and believe in Jesus, their name is now written in and recorded in the Lamb's Book of Life.

King David said in Psalm 139:13–18, "For Thou didst form my inward parts; Thou didst weave me in my mother's womb. I will give thanks to Thee, for I am fearfully and wonderfully made; wonderful are Thy works, and my soul knows it very well. My frame was not hidden from Thee, when I was made in secret, and skillfully made in the depths of the earth. Your eyes have seen my unformed substance; and in Thy book they were all written, the days that were ordained for me, when as yet there was not one of them. How precious also are Thy thoughts to me, O God! How vast is the sum of them! If I should count them, they would outnumber the sand. When I awake I am still with Thee."

"Nevertheless do not rejoice in this, that the spirits are subject to you, but rejoice that your names are recorded in heaven" (Luke 10:20).

"But you have come to Mount Zion and to the city of the living God, the heavenly Jerusalem, and to myriads of angels, to the general assembly and church of the first-born who are _enrolled in heaven,_ and to God, the Judge of all, and to the spirits of righteous men made perfect, and to Jesus, the mediator of a new covenant, and to the sprinkled blood, which speaks better than the blood of Abel" (Hebrews 12: 22–24). This is how it is when we are truly born again.

"His divine power has granted to us everything pertaining to life and godliness, through the true knowledge of Him who called us by His own glory and excellence. For by these God has granted to us His precious and magnificent promises, in order that by them you might become partakers of the divine nature, having escaped the corruption that is in the world by lust" (2 Peter 1:3, 4).

John said that he saw many books in heaven, and I believe the books, other than the Book of Life, were books that have recorded everything that all of mankind has done and said throughout their lives here on earth.

In Exodus 32:32, 33, when Moses asked God to forgive the people of their sin, he said, "But now, if Thou will forgive their sin - - - and if not, please blot me out from Thy book which Thou has written. And the Lord said to Moses, whoever has sinned against Me, I will blot him out of My book."

In Revelation 5:1, John says, "I saw in the right hand of Him who sat on the throne, a book written inside and on the back, sealed with seven seals. Only Jesus, the Lamb, was worthy to open the book with seven seals."

"By this, love is perfected in us, that we may have confidence in the day of judgment; because as He is in heaven, so also are we in this world (perfect)" (1 John 4:17).

"And I saw the dead, the great and small, standing before the throne, and book's were opened; and another book was opened which is the Book of Life; and the dead were judged from the things that were written in the book's according to their deeds. And if anyone's name was not found written in the the Book of Life, he was thrown into the lake of fire" (Revelation 20:12).

"But if we judged ourselves rightly, we should not be judged. But when we are judged, we are disciplined by the Lord in order that we may not be condemned along with the world" (1 Corinthians 11:31–33).

In Revelation 3:5, Jesus said, "He who overcomes shall thus be clothed in white garments; and I will not erase his name from the Book of Life, and I will confess (proclaim, exalt) his name before My Father and His angels."

1. *A remnant prepared*—"And it will come about that he who is left in Zion and remains in Jerusalem, will be called holy—and everyone who is recorded for life in Jerusalem" (Isaiah 4:3). This life means to live forever.

2. *The time of the end*—"Now at that time, Michael the great prince who stands guard over the son's of your people will arise. And there will be a time of distress such as never occurred since there was a nation until that time, and at that time; Your people, everyone who is found written in the Book of Life, will be rescued. And many of those who sleep in the dust of the ground will awake, these to everlasting life,

but the others, to disgrace and everlasting contempt" (Daniel 12:1–2).

3. *The book of remembrance*—"Then those who revered the Lord, spoke to one another, and the Lord gave attention and heard it, and a Book of Remembrance was written before Him, for those who revere the Lord and who esteem His name. So, He will distinguish between the righteous and the wicked, one who serves God and one who does not serve Him" (Malachi 3:16–18).

The New Jerusalem and New Earth

The Apostle John in his vision and being caught up into heaven and saw the very end of our story here on earth, which is to be a new beginning for all eternity.

And I saw a new heaven and a new earth; for the first heaven and first earth passed away, and there is no longer any sea. And I saw the holy city, the new Jerusalem, coming down out of heaven from God, made ready as a bride adorned for her husband. And I heard a loud voice from the throne, saying, "Behold, the tabernacle of God is among men, and He shall dwell and live among them, and they shall be His people, and God Himself shall be among them, and He shall wipe away every tear from their eyes; and there shall no longer be any death; and there shall no longer be any mourning, or crying, or pain; the first things have passed away."

And He who sits on the throne said, "Behold, I am making all things new." And He said, "Write, for these words are faithful and true." And He said to me, "It is done. I am the Alpha, and the Omega, the beginning and the end (in Hebrew, "I am the Aleph, and the Taw"). I will give to the one who thirsts from the spring of the water of life without cost" (in Hebrew "*Mayim Heiym*"). He who overcomes shall inherit these things, and I will be his God and he shall be my son. (Revelation 21:1–7).

"But for the cowardly and unbelieving and abominable and murderers and immoral persons and sorcerers and idolaters and all liars, their part will be in the lake that burns with fire and brimstone, which is the second death" (Revelation 21:8).

"And nothing unclean and no one who practices abomination and lying shall ever come into it, but only those whose names are written in the Lamb's Book of Life" (Revelation 21:27). Amen!

21

Questions about Heaven and Eternity

Will we have bodies in heaven?

If not, why did God give the saints in heaven robes of white if they didn't have bodies? (Revelation 6:10, 11). Our body and spirit will reunite at Christ's second coming (1 Corinthians 15:48, 49). We will be just like him, a supernatural being.

In John 20:20, 21, 27, when Jesus appeared to the apostles in the upper room eight days after his resurrection from the dead, they thought he was a ghost or spirit. He showed them both his hands and side that had been pierced on the cross of love. Thomas was not with them at that time, and he breathed on them and said, "Receive the Holy Spirit." A week later, his disciples were inside, and Thomas who doubted them a week earlier was there, and Jesus said to him, "Reach here your finger and see my hands and reach here your hand and put it into my side. And be not unbelieving but believing." Then Thomas said to him, "My Lord and my God."

"See My hands and My feet, that it is I Myself; touch Me and see, for a ghost does not have flesh and bones as you see that I have" (Luke 24:37–43). The door was locked or shut when

Jesus appeared to them in bodily form, but he was also a Spirit being. He entered the room invisibly and materialized to them like on *Star Trek*—"Beam me up or down, Scotty." Everyone that Jesus appeared to for forty days after his resurrection from the dead, he appeared to in bodily form. Otherwise, they would not have been able to see him with their physical eyes.

In Acts 1:9, Jesus was lifted up while they were looking on, and a cloud received him out of their sight. This tells me that Jesus went up into heaven in bodily form.

Will we go immediately to heaven?

Yes, in Psalm 146:4, the Spirit departs from the body, and the body returns to the earth. In 1 Corinthians 13:12, we will know just as we have also been fully known. The Bible says that the saints, those who have gone before us, are in heaven right now, cheering us on. Your grandparents, your father or mother, brothers and sisters, friends, etc.—these are the saints in heaven.

Will we have emotions?

Yes, because emotions are a part of the soul. The Bible says, "There is great joy in heaven when a sinner repents." But we will not remember all the pain, sorrow, and suffering that we might have had on earth; only the joyful and good things.

Will we know everything?

No, we will not know everything as God does, but we will remember things of when we were on earth. In Revelation, it says, "And the dead martyrs said, when will you avenge our blood, Lord?"

Will we know what's happening on earth?

Yes, it says in Hebrews 12:1 that there is a great cloud of witnesses in heaven that are cheering you on.

Will we remember our life on earth?

Yes, Abraham said, "Son, remember your life on earth."

Will we know people in heaven?

Yes!

Will it be boring in heaven?

No, but Satan wants you to think so. Heaven will be like a continuous, awesome, joyful party full of only happiness. The Bible says that what the eye has not seen or the ear has not heard of is what's in store for us Christians in heaven. It will be absolute joy and bliss.

We will not spend eternity in heaven because in Revelation 21, John saw the New Jerusalem coming down from heaven to the new earth. God will live and dwell there with us forever.

Who will be there?

All those who died believing in Jesus, whose names were written in the Lamb's Book of Life (Romans 10:13; Revelation 21:16, 17). "I will give eternal life to whoever desires to be saved" (John 10:28, 17:23; Romans 2:7, 6:23).

About the Author

I was born ten days after the bombing of Pearl Harbor in 1941, in La Crosse, Wisconsin. I was born three months premature, and the doctor told my mother, "Take him home. He's not going to survive." My mother was a very strong woman of faith and said, "There is no way that God who gave this son to me is going to let him die." My lungs were very weak, and she put Indian remedies, poultice bags on my chest with herbs and such and with heat. And from then on, I was a momma's boy.

Our family of five at that time moved to Oregon in 1951, and I grew up in Portland. My family was, as a lot of families are, very dysfunctional. My mother was raised a Roman Catholic, but she read the Bible for herself and sent us to churches that were near our home. I eventually had two brothers and four sisters. My oldest sister still lives with her family in the La Crosse, Wisconsin area.

I think that the Holy Spirit of God touched my heart when I was in the seventh grade, and I became a born-again Christian. I fell away and did my own thing for many years, but I never let go of God, and I know that he never let go of me.

When I was forty years old and married to my second wife, the Lord was prompting me to totally and forever surrender my life to him. I made a totally new commitment and was rebaptized in 1982. I determined to read the Bible all the way through, and since then I have read eight different translations of the Bible all the way through. I also love to study the Aramaic, Hebrew, and Greek for insight and knowledge from my best friend and teacher, the Holy Spirit of my Father God.

The Lord and his love for me is the only source of all that I am and will ever be. I am my beloved's, and he is mine.

CPSIA information can be obtained
at www.ICGtesting.com
Printed in the USA
FFHW021002230119
50273546-55284FF

9 781641 914079